The Fourfold Gospel

A.B. Simpson

The Fourfold Gospel

ALBERT B. SIMPSON'S CONCEPTION

OF THE COMPLETE PROVISION OF CHRIST

FOR EVERY NEED OF THE BELIEVER . . .

SPIRIT, SOUL AND BODY.

UPDATED AND EDITED.

CHRISTIAN PUBLICATIONS
Camp Hill, Pennsylvania

✝ *The mark of vibrant faith*

Christian Publications, Inc.
Publishing House of The Christian and Missionary Alliance
3825 Hartzdale Drive, Camp Hill, PA 17011

Library of Congress Catalog Card No. 84-70151
© 1984 by Christian Publications. All rights reserved
ISBN: 0-87509-347-7
Printed in the United States of America

Cover photo: Steve Miller

Contents

Introduction

The original title of this little volume, *The Fourfold Gospel,* has become a familiar phrase to thousands of God's children. Not that the truths contained in the statement were unknown before, but the grouping of them in this form was given to Dr. A.B. Simpson, founder of The Christian and Missionary Alliance, after he had happily experienced the fullness of the gospel in his own life.

This does not mean that the blessings of the gospel are limited exclusively to four—Christ our Savior, Christ our Sanctifier, Christ our Healer and Christ our Coming King. In one sense it is a manifold gospel with countless blessings and ever deeper and richer experiences of God's grace and love. "But there are four messages in the gospel," says the author, "which sum up in a very complete way the blessings which Christ has to offer us and which it is especially important that Christians should emphasize today." These constitute four great pillars in the temple of truth.

Note the order of these great truths. First things first—Christ our Savior. Rightly, the first has to do with the soul, lost through sin and estrangement from God, but "made nigh by the blood of Christ." It is no small thing to be saved—justified, forgiven, born again. This foundation truth needs to be reiterated in these days when sin is minimized or explained away and the atonement of Jesus Christ is rejected by many. The same is true of sanctification—a word and experience misunderstood and evaded by many believers. It marks a definite and distinct crisis in the life of a person. The unfolding of these four phases of the gospel will be made fascinatingly clear to the reader of this book. It is worthy of thoughtful and prayerful study, and best of all of appropriating the full-orbed message—the all-sufficient Christ for spirit, soul and body.

Dr. Simpson proved this in his own life; otherwise, his preaching would have been in vain, The Christian and Missionary Alliance would not have come into existence, and multiplied thousands of people the world around would have been deprived of the knowledge and experience of a complete Christ. Addressing an audience in London many years ago, Dr. Simpson related the following experiences which marked three great epochs in his life: "Some twenty-seven years ago, I floundered for ten months in the waters of despondency, and I got out of them just by believing in Jesus as my Savior. About twelve years ago I fell into another deep experience of conviction, and I got out of that by believing in Jesus as my Sanctifier. After years of teaching and waiting on Him, the Lord Jesus Christ showed me four years ago that it was His blessed will to be my complete Savior for body as well as soul."

This exposition has had a very large circulation in

past years. Nothing better, outside of the Bible, could be put in the hands of converts. One of our evangelists in the earlier years of the work used hundreds of them in that way with marked results.

The message is simple, scriptural and satisfying. The Church needs it as antidote to error and apostasy, a sure remedy for failure, an answer to the cry of hungry hearts, a source of health for the body and an inspiration to complete the witness and bring back the King.

Frederic H. Senft

1

Christ Our Savior

And cried with a loud voice, saying, Salvation to our God which sitteth upon the throne, and unto the Lamb (Revelation 7:10).

Salvation is the cry of the ransomed around the throne when the universe is dissolving in wreckage and terror is filling the hearts of men. It is the first cry of the ransomed after they reach their home and have seen all that it means to be lost and to be saved, while the earth is reeling, and the elements are melting, and all things are quaking and trembling in the first approaches of the great catastrophe.

They see behind them all the way through which the Lord has led them. Down that long vista they behold the toils they have come through and the perils they have escaped. They recognize how tenderly the grace of God has led them on and kept them safe. They see the robes and crowns that are prepared for them and all the joy of the eternal future which is opening before them. They see all this, and then they behold Him whose hand has kept it all safely for them, and whose heart has chosen it for them.

They look back upon all the past; they look forward into all the future; they look up into the face of Him to whom it was all due. And then they lift up their voices in one glad exultant cry: "Salvation to our God which sitteth upon the throne, and unto the Lamb." This is what salvation means; this is what they have believed for; this is what He died to give them. They have it all. They are saved and the full realization of it has come home to their hearts at last.

Let us look a little at what it means to be saved. It is not at all a little thing. We sometimes hear that certain Christians are *only* justified. It is a mighty thing to be justified. It is a glorious thing to be born again. Christ said it was greater to have one's name written in heaven than to be able to cast out devils. What does salvation mean?

WHAT WE ARE SAVED FROM

1. Salvation takes away the guilt of sin. It frees us from all liability and punishment for past offences. Sin deserves punishment. Salvation takes this all away. Is it not glorious to be saved?

2. Salvation saves us from the wrath of God. God hates evil and must punish it somehow. The wrath of God is revealed from heaven against all unrighteousness of men. But salvation delivers us from this.

3. Salvation delivers us from the curse of the law. We can recall the terrors of the law's revealing, the lightning and thunder that surrounded the mountain, and the terror of Israel before it was given at all.

They could not bear that God should speak to them thus, and they entreated Moses, "Speak thou with us and we will hear; but let not God speak with us, lest we die."

But if the giving of the law was terrible, more terrible was its breaking. It is perilous to break the law of the land. The most tender appeal of affection does not avail to save the condemned criminal. Justice must be satisfied.

When the assassin of President Lincoln was stalking through the land, the law would have searched the world to find him. How terrible it must have been for him to feel that the eye of justice was looking for him and sooner or later would surely find him! The circle narrowed and narrowed around him till at last he was grasped in the cordon. So the cordon of law tightens around the sinner who is under its power. Salvation delivers us from this curse through Him who was made a curse for us.

4. It delivers us also from our evil consciences. There is always a shadow left on our hearts by sin and a feeling of remorse. It is the black wing of the raven, and its hoarse voice is ever whispering of despair. The memory of past guilt will follow people so that after many years they tell of crimes committed, the punishment for which they escaped, but the burden of which never left their consciences. Perhaps it seemed to slumber for a while, but at last it sprang upon them like a lion. Salvation delivers us from our evil consciences. It takes the shadow from the heart and the stinging memory of sin from the soul.

5. It delivers us from an evil heart which is the source of all the sin in the life. It is natural for men to

sin even while they hate it. The tendency toward evil is in every nature, chained to it like a body of death so that even when we want to do good, evil is present with us. It takes possession of the will and heart like a living death. It is offensive, it smells of the sepulcher, it is full of the poison of asps, it putrefies the whole moral being and bears it down to death. Salvation frees us from its power and gives us a new nature.

6. It frees us from the fear of death. It takes away the sting of that last enemy, through fear of whom we would otherwise all our lifetime be subject to bondage. I remember when I was a child what a shock a funeral bell would give me. I could not bear to hear of someone being dead. The love of Christ has taken this all away. The deathbed of God's children is to them the portal of heaven.

7. Salvation delivers us from Satan's power and kingdom. God has "delivered us from the power of darkness and translated us into the kingdom of His dear Son." We are saved from the ills and the serpent and the bonds of sin, and the devil is a conquered foe. Salvation delivers us from much sorrow and distress in life. It brings a glorious sunlight into life and drives away those clouds of depression and gloom which overwhelm us.

8. Beyond all else, salvation delivers us from eternal death. We are not going down into outer darkness and the depths of woe. Christ has unlocked the fetters of the pit and saved us from endless death. We are delivered from that terrible agony which the kindest lips that ever spoke has called the "worm that dieth not, and the fire that is not quenched."

These are some of the things that salvation has

delivered us from. Is it not indeed glad tidings?

WHAT SALVATION BRINGS TO US

1. Salvation brings the forgiveness of all our sins and entirely removes them. They are blotted out as completely as though we had paid all that was due for them, and they can never appear against us again.

2. Salvation brings us justification in the sight of God so that we stand before Him as righteous beings. We are accepted as though we had done everything He had commanded and had perfectly kept the law in every particular. With one stroke of the pen He erases the account that was against us; with another stroke He puts there all the righteousness of Christ.

We must accept both sides of this. The spotlessness of Jesus is put to our accounts as if it were our own. All His obedience to the Father is ours. All His patience and gentleness are ours. Every service that He has rendered to bless others is put to our accounts as if we had done it all. Every good thing we can discover in Him is ours, and every evil thing in us is His. That is salvation. Is it not wonderful?

3. Salvation brings us into the favor and love of God and secures for us full acceptance in the person of Jesus. He loves us as He loves His only begotten Son. The moment we are presented in the arms of Christ we are accepted in Him.

Dr. Currie, a brilliant Methodist writer and editor of one of the best journals of his church, dreamed one night that he died and went up to the gate of heaven. There he met an angel and asked to be allowed to enter. The angel asked him who he was.

"I am Dr. Currie," he answered, "editor of the

Quarterly Review of the Methodist Episcopal Church." The angel replied, "I don't know you; I never heard of you before." Soon he met another angel and told him the same story, and received the same answer: "I don't know you."

At last one of the angels said, "Let us go to the Judge and see if He will know you." He went before the throne and told the Judge about his life and the work he had done for the church, but received the answer from the Judge: "I don't know you at all." His heart was beginning to gather the blackness of despair, when suddenly there was One at his side with a crown of thorns upon His head.

"Father," this One said, "I know him. I will answer for him." And instantly all the harps of heaven began to sing: "Worthy is the Lamb that was slain," and he was ushered into all the glory of the celestial world. Not all the preaching we have done, or all the service we have rendered will amount to anything there. We must be identified with the Man who wore the thorns; we must be accepted in the Beloved, and then the Father will love us even as He loves His Son. We shall stand with Him even as Christ does.

4. Salvation gives us a new heart. It brings to us regeneration of the soul. Every spark of life from the old polluted nature is worthless, and the divine nature is born in us as a part of our very being.

5. Salvation gives us grace to live day by day. A man may be pardoned and released from prison, but have no money to supply his needs. He is pardoned, yet he is starving. Salvation takes us out of prison, and provides for all our needs besides. It enables us to

rejoice in God, who "is able to keep [us] from falling, and to present [us] faultless before the presence of his glory with exceeding joy."

6. Salvation brings to us the help of the Holy Spirit, ever at our side as a gentle mother, helping our infirmities and bringing grace for every time of need.

7. Salvation brings to us the care of God's providence, causing all things to work together for our good. This is never true until we are saved; but when we are the children of God, all things in earth and in heaven are on our side.

8. Salvation opens the way for all the blessings that follow it. It is the steppingstone to sanctification and healing, and the peace that passes understanding. From this first gateway the prospect opens boundlessly to all the good land we may go on to possess.

9. Salvation brings to us eternal life. It is, of course, only the beginning, but the heavenly land has its portals open even here, and when we at last reach the throne and look out and see all the possibilities that yet lie before us, we shall sing with the ransomed, "Salvation to our God which sitteth upon the throne, and unto the Lamb."

THE PROCESS OF THESE BLESSINGS

1. These blessings come through the mercy and grace of God. "God so loved the world, that he gave his only begotton Son, that whosoever believeth in him should not perish, but have everlasting life."

2. Salvation comes to us by the righteousness of Jesus Christ. He perfectly fulfilled every requirement of the law. Had He faltered in one temptation we could not have been saved. Think of that when

you are tempted to speak a hasty word. Suppose Jesus had done so. We could have been lost forever. Every moment He held steadfastly in the path of obedience, and His perfect grace and obedience are the price of our salvation.

3. Salvation comes to us through the death of Christ. His obedience is not enough. He must die. His crucifixion is the atonement for our sins.

4. Salvation comes through the resurrection of Jesus Christ from the dead, which was God's seal of His accomplished work and the pledge of our pardon.

5. Salvation comes through the intercession of Jesus at the right hand of the Father. He is our Great High Priest there, where He ever lives to make intercession for us, and thus keeps us in continual acceptance.

6. Salvation comes through the grace of the Holy Spirit. The Spirit of God is sent down, through the intercession of Christ, to carry out in our hearts and lives His work. He keeps our feet in the way, and He will never leave His work until He has put us forever into the bosom of Jesus.

7. Salvation comes to us by the gospel. It is presented to us through this message and our refusal to accept it, or our neglect to do so, fixes irrevocably, by our own act, our eternal condition. If we are saved, we become so by accepting the gospel, which is called "the gospel of your salvation."

THE STEPS TO SALVATION

1. Conviction of sin is the first step. We must see our need and our danger before we can be saved. The Holy Spirit brings this to our heart and conscience.

Until there is this knowledge of the need of Christ, He cannot be received; but when the heart is deeply impressed under a sense of sin, Christ is precious indeed.

2. There must be next an apprehension of Jesus as our Savior. We must see Him as both able and willing to save. It will not do merely to feel and confess our guilt. We need to focus our eyes on Jesus. So Christ says to every seeking soul, "Look! Look! Look unto Me and be saved!" "Every one which seeth the Son, and believeth on him, may have everlasting life."

3. Salvation comes by repentance. There must be a turning from sin. This does not consist of mere emotional feeling necessarily, but it does mean to have the whole will and purpose of heart turned from sin to God.

4. Salvation comes by coming to Jesus. We must do more than turn away from sin. That alone will not save us. Lot's wife turned away from Sodom—but she was not in Zoar. There must be a turning to Jesus as well as a turning from sin.

5. Salvation comes by accepting Jesus as the Savior. This does not mean merely crying out to Him to save, but claiming Him as the Savior, embracing the promises He has given, and so believing that He is our personal Redeemer.

6. Salvation comes by believing that Christ has accepted us, and counting Him faithful who has promised. This will bring the sweetness of assurance and peace, and as we believe the promise, the Spirit will seal it to our hearts and witness that we are the children of God.

7. Salvation comes by confessing Christ as the Savior. This is a necessary step. It is like the ratification of a deed or the celebration of a marriage; it stamps and seals our act of commitment.

8. Salvation involves our abiding in Jesus. Having taken it for a fact, once for all, that we are saved, we must never do the work over again. "As ye have, therefore, received Christ Jesus the Lord, so walk ye in Him."

WHAT THE BIBLE SAYS ABOUT SALVATION

1. It is called God's salvation. It was not invented by man. God alone is the author of it, and He is the only Savior.

2. It is also called "your own salvation," because we ourselves must appropriate it.

3. It is called "the common salvation," because it is free to all who will accept it.

4. It is called a "great salvation," because it is full and infinite in its provisions. It is large enough for all our needs.

5. Christ is called the "mighty to save," because no matter how weak or how wicked we sinners may be, He is able to save us to the uttermost.

6. It is called a near salvation. "Say not in thine heart, Who shall ascend into heaven? (that is, to bring Christ down from above;) Or, Who shall descend into the deep? (that is, to bring up Christ again from the dead.) But what saith it? The word is nigh thee, *even* in thy mouth, and in thy heart: that is, the word of faith, which we preach: That if thou shalt confess with thy mouth the Lord Jesus, and shalt believe in thine heart that God hath raised him from

the dead, thou shalt be saved" (Romans 10:6-9).

We do not have to get up into some exalted state to find Christ, or down into some profound and terrible experience. We can find Him everywhere we are. Salvation is at our door. We can take it as we find Him very near to us. No steps were allowed to God's ancient altar, for then some poor sinner might not be able to get up to it. Jesus is on the very plane where we are this moment. We can take His salvation here now. We can take Him as we are, and He will lead us into all the experiences we need.

WHY IT IS CALLED GOOD NEWS

1. It is called good news because of its value. It comes laden with blessings to us who receive it.

2. It is called good news because of its freedom. It may be taken without money and without price.

3. It is called good news because of its availability. It is easy of access, being on the level of the worst sinner.

4. It is called good news because of its universality. Whosoever will may take it and live.

5. It is called good news because of the security of its blessings. They are given forevermore. "Verily, verily, I say unto you, He that heareth my word, and believeth on him that sent me, hath everlasting life, and shall not come into condemnation."

6. It is called good news because of the eternity of its blessings. The sun will have burnt itself into ashes, the earth will have been destroyed by intense heat, the heavens will be changed when salvation has only begun. Then a thousand times ten thousand years shall pass, and we shall have only begun a

little to understand what salvation means. Blessed
be God for the gospel of Christ's salvation.

WHY WE SHOULD RECEIVE AND
SHARE THIS SALVATION

1. Every man's salvation hinges upon his own
choice and free will. It is an awful thing to have the
power to take salvation and to throw that oppor-
tunity away. And yet it is left to our choice. We are
not forced to take it. We must voluntarily choose it
or reject it.

2. The salvation of our souls is a tremendous responsibility for which we are held accountable. God
has put salvation into our hands as a jewel of inesti-
mable value, and He will hold us to a strict account
for the way we treat this precious thing. If we destroy it, how fearful will be our doom when we meet
the Judge of all the earth, and hear the stern question from His lips, "Where is thy soul?"

3. Guilt will rest upon us if we neglect and de-
spise the precious blood of Christ shed for our salvation. To neglect it is to throw it away. He has provided a great salvation. If it is worth so much to man,
if it has cost God so much to provide it, what can be
thought of him who makes little of it? Jesus suffered
intensely to bring salvation to us, and shall we stumble carelessly over it? Oh, let us be more concerned
than we are, both for the salvation of our own souls
and for those around us who are not saved.

4. The little word "now" is always linked with
salvation. Salvation must be taken now or never.
The cycle of life is very narrow. We do not know
how soon it will end. "Behold, now is the day of

salvation.''

5. Salvation's issues are for eternity. The decisions there are not reversible. We cannot come back from death and have another chance to secure salvation. When once the Master has risen up and shut the door, we will find we have been left out forever. The cry will then be, "I have lost my chance; it is too late." God's Word holds out no second chance.

6. If salvation is missed there will be no excuse for it. Not one thing has been left undone in presenting salvation to men. God's best thought and Christ's best love have been given to it. All has been done that could be done. Salvation has been brought down to our level. It has been placed where we can reach it.

God has provided all the resources, even the grace, repentance and faith, if we will take them. If we lack anything, God will put His arms around us and lift us up to Him, breathing His faith into us, and carrying us Himself until we are able to walk. Salvation is brought to every sinner. If we are lost it is because we have neglected and defied God's love.

Although we proclaim this salvation, eternity will be too short to tell it all. We must take it and then go out and gather others in to share it. We will receive glorious crowns, but the best of it all will be that men and women will be saved.

In New York City, hanging expensively framed in a parlor is a little bit of paper—a telegraph form. On it is just one word: SAVED!

The cablegram was framed by the lady of that mansion, because it is dearer to her than all her works of art. One day when the awful news came to her through the papers that the ship on which her husband had sailed was wrecked, that little message came to her door and saved her from despair. It was the message of that rescued man, and it meant to two hearts all that life is worth.

Oh, let such a message go up today to yonder shore. The Holy Spirit will flash it hence while I am drawing the next breath. The angels will echo it over heaven, and there are dear friends there to whom it will mean as much as their own very heaven.

I have seen another short sentence in a frame, too. It came from one who had been rescued from a ship where friends and family had all perished. Those dear little ones were in the slimy caves of the cruel sea. Those beloved faces had gone down forever, but he was saved, and from yonder shore he sent back this sad and weary message: SAVED ALONE!

So I can imagine a selfish Christian entering yonder portals. They meet him at the gates. "Where are your dear ones?" "Where are your friends?" "Where is your crown?" "Alas, I am saved alone." God help you, reader, to so receive and give, that you shall save yourself and others also.

> *Must I go, and empty handed,*
> *Must I thus my Savior meet,*
> *Not one soul with which to greet Him,*
> *Lay no trophy at His feet?*

2

Christ Our Sanctifier

And for their sakes I sanctify myself, that they also might be sanctified through the truth (John 17:19).

The marginal reading of the last clause is, "that they also might be truly sanctified." This seems to imply that there is something which passes in the world for holiness, which is not true sanctification. There are counterfeit forms of Christian life, and also defective forms, which do not represent all that the fullness of Christ is able to do for us. Sanctification is the second step in the fourfold gospel.

WHAT SANCTIFICATION IS NOT

There are good elements and even holy elements in Christian character which are not sanctification.
1. Sanctification is not regeneration. It is not conversion. It is a great and blessed thing to become a Christian. It is never a matter of small account. To be saved eternally is cause for eternal joy; but the soul

must also enter into sanctification. They are not the same. Regeneration is the beginning. It is the germ of the seed, but it is not the summer fullness of the plant. The heart has not yet gained entire victory over the old elements of sin. It is sometimes overcome by them.

Regeneration is like building a house and having the work done well. Sanctification is having the owner come and dwell in the house and fill it with gladness and life and beauty. Many Christians are converted and stop there. They do not go on to the fullness of their life in Christ, and so are in danger of losing what they already possess.

Germany brought in the grand truth of justification by faith, through the teachings of Martin Luther, but he failed to go on to the deeper teachings of the Christian life. What was the result? Germany today is cold and lifeless and the very hotbed of rationalism and all its attendant evils. How different it has been in England! The labors of men like Wesley and Baxter and Whitfield, who understood the mission of the Holy Spirit, have led the Christian life of England and America, her offspring, into deeper and more permanent channels.

Men and women who do not press on in their Christian experience to gain the fullness of their inheritance in Him will often become cold and formal. The evil in their own heart will assert itself again and may very likely overcome them, and their work will bring confusion and disaster to the cause of Christ. If they escape the result, it will be as by fire.

You have doubtless noticed young Christians who have seemed to be marvelously converted and filled with the love of God, but they have not entered into the deeper life of Christ and in an evil hour they failed. They had gained a new heart, but they had neglected to get the deeper teaching and life which Christ has for all His children.

2. Sanctification is not morality, or any attainment of character. There is very much that is lovely in human life which is not sanctification. A man cannot build up a good human character himself and then call it the work of God. It will not stand the strain that is sure to come upon it. Only the house that is founded upon the Rock of Ages will abide securely in the wrath of the elements.

3. Sanctification is not your own work; it is not a gradual attainment which you can grow into by your own efforts. If you should be able to build such a structure yourself, and add to it year after year until it was completed, would you not then stand off with a pardonable pride and look upon it as your own work? No, you cannot grow into sanctification.

You will grow after you are in sanctification into a fuller, riper and more mature development of life in Christ, but you must take it at its commencement as a gift, not as a growth. It is an obtainment, not an attainment. You cannot sanctify yourself. The only thing to do is to give yourself wholly to God, a voluntary sacrifice. This is intensely important. It is but a light thing to do for Him. But He must do the work of cleansing and filling.

4. Sanctification is not the work of death. It is strange that anyone should think there could be a sanctifying influence in the dying struggle. Yet many have lived in that delusion for years. People expect

that the cold sweat of that last hour and the con-
vulsive throbbing of the sinking heart will somehow
place them in the arms of their Sanctifier. This comes
in some degree from the old idea that their sin is
seated in the body—the old Manichaen teaching that
the flesh is unholy, and if we were once rid of the
body, the fleshless tenant would be free from sin and
would spring at once into boundless purity.

There is no sin in these bones and flesh and liga-
ments. If you cast off your hand you have lost no sin.
If both hands are gone you are as sinful as ever. If you
cut off your head and yield up your life, sin would
still remain in the soul. Sin is not in the body, it is
in the heart and the soul and the will. Divest yourself
of this body of clay, and the spirit will still be left, a
hard, rebellious, sinful thing. Death will not sanctify
it. It is a poor time to be converted. It will be a poorer
time to be sanctified.

I would not advise any one to put off his or her salvation to the dying hour, when the heart is oppressed
and the brain clouded and the mind has need of confidence and rest and a sense of victory to enable it to
enter into His presence with fullness of joy. Nor is it
a better time for the deeper work of the Holy Spirit.
Sanctification should be entered into intelligently
when the mind is clear. It is a deliberate act calling
for the calm exercise of all the faculties working
under the controlling influence of the Divine Spirit.

5. Sanctification is not self-perfection. We shall
never become so inherently good that there will be
no possibility or temptation to sin. We shall never
reach a place where we shall not need to abide in
Him each moment. The instant we feel able to live

without Him, there comes up a separate life within us which is not a sanctified life.

The reason the exalted spirits in heaven fell from their high estate was, perhaps, because they became conscious of their own beauty, and pride arose in their hearts. They looked at themselves, and became as gods unto themselves. The moment you or I become conscious that we are strong or pure, that instant the work of disintegration begins. It has made us independent of Him, and we have separated ourselves from the life of Christ. We must be simple, empty vessels, open channels for His life to flow through. Then Christ's perfection will be imparted to us. And we shall grow less and less in ourselves, as He becomes more and more within us.

6. Sanctification is not a state of emotion. It is not an ecstasy or a sensation. It resides in the will and purpose of life. It is a practical conformity of life and conduct to the will and character of God. The will must choose God. The purpose of the heart must be to yield to Him, to please and obey Him. That is the important thing: to love, to choose and to do His holy will. You cannot have that spirit in you and fail to be happy. The spirit that craves mere sensational joy has yet an unholy self-life. It must get out of that form of self and into God before it can receive much from Him.

WHAT SANCTIFICATION IS

Let us look at the positive side.

1. Sanctification is separation from sin. That is the root idea of the word. The sanctified Christian is separated from sin, from an evil world, even from his

own self and from anything that would be a separating cause between him and Christ in the new life.

Sanctification does not mean that sin and Satan are to be destroyed. God does not yet bring the millennium, but He puts a line of demarcation between the sanctified soul and all that is unholy. The great trouble with Christians is they try to destroy evil. They think if sin could be really decapitated and Satan slain they would be supremely happy.

It is a surprise to many persons after conversion that God still lets the devil live. He has nowhere promised that He will kill Satan, but He has promised to put a broad, deep Jordan between the Christian and sin. The only thing to do with sin is to repudiate it and let it alone. There is sin enough in the world to destroy us all if we take it in. The air is full of it, as air can be full of soot from the soft coal that is burned. It will be so to the end of time, but God means you and me to be separated from sin in our spirit.

2. Sanctification means also dedication to God. That is a root idea of the word also. It is separation from sin and dedication unto God. A sanctified Christian is wholly yielded to God to please Him in every particular. His first thought always is, "Thy will be done." His one desire is that he may please God and do His holy will. This is the thought expressed by the word consecration.

In the Old Testament all things which were set apart to God were called sanctified, even if there had been no sin in them before. The tabernacle was sanctified; it had never sinned, but it was dedicated to God. In the same sense all the vessels of the tabernacle were sanctified. They were set apart to a holy use. God expects something more of us than simply to be separated from sin. That is only negative goodness. He expects that we shall be wholly dedicated to Him, having it the supreme wish of our heart to love and honor and please Him. Are we fulfilling His expectations in this?

3. Sanctification includes conformity to the likeness of God. We are to be in His image, and stamped with the impress of Jesus Christ.

4. Sanctification means conformity also to the will as well as the likeness of God. A sanctified Christian is submissive and obedient. He desires the Divine will above everything else in life as kinder and wiser for him than anything else can be. He is conscious that he misses something if he misses it. He knows it will promote his highest good far more than his own will, crying instinctively, "Thy will be done."

> Thou sweet, beloved will of God,
> On thee I lay me down and rest,
> As babe upon its mother's breast.

5. Sanctification means love, supreme love to God and all mankind. This is the fulfilling of the law. It is the spring of all obedience, the fountain from which all right things flow. We cannot be conformed to the image of God without love, for God is love.

This is, perhaps, the strongest feature in a truly sanctified life. It clothes all the other virtues with softness and warmth. It takes the icy peaks of a cold and naked consecration and covers them with mosses and verdure. It sends bright sunlight into the heart, making everything warm and full of life, which would otherwise be cold and desolate. The savage was able to stand before his enemies and be cut to pieces with stoical firmness that disdained to cry, but his indifference was like some stony cliff. It was not the warm, tender love of the heart of Jesus which made Him bow meekly to His painful death because it was His Father's will. It was the spontaneous, glad outflowing of His loving heart.

If we are so filled with love to God, it will flow out to others, and we shall love our neighbors as we love ourselves.

THE SOURCE OF SANCTIFICATION

The heart and soul of the whole matter is seeing that Jesus is himself our sanctification. We must not look at it merely as some great mountain peak where He is standing and which we have to climb, but between us and it there are almost inaccessible cliffs to ascend before we can stand at His side.

Jesus himself becomes our sanctification. "For their sakes I sanctify myself, that they also might be sanctified." It seems as though He was a little afraid His followers would begin to look for sanctification apart from Himself, and knowing that it could never reach them except through Him, He said, "I sanctify myself" (John 17:19).

1. He has purchased it for us. It is part of the fruit of Calvary. By one offering He hath perfected forever them that are sanctified. "By the which will we are sanctified through the offering of the body of Jesus Christ once *for all*" (Hebrews 10:10).

2. Sanctification does not come to us by our efforts, but it is made available to us as the purchase of His

death upon the cross. It is ours by the purchase of Jesus just as much as forgiveness is. You have as much right to be holy and sanctified as you have to be saved. You can go to God and claim it as your inheritance as much as you can your pardon for sin. If you do not have it you are falling short of your redemption privileges.

3. Sanctification is to be received as one of the free gifts God desires to bestow upon us. If it is not a gift, then it is not a part of redemption. If it is a part of redemption, then it is as free as the blood of Jesus.

4. Sanctification comes through the personal indwelling of Jesus. He does not put righteousness into the heart simply, but He comes there personally Himself to live. Words are weak; they, indeed, are utterly inadequate to express this thought. When we arrive at complete despair of all other ways we learn this truth. Jesus Christ himself comes into the heart and lives His own life there and so becomes the sanctification of the soul.

This is the meaning of the text. It is to His people that Jesus sanctifies himself, and any who try to live a sanctified life apart from Him are not truly sanctified. They must take Jesus in as their life to be truly sanctified. That is the personal sense of divine holiness. "But of him are ye in Christ Jesus, who of God is made unto us wisdom, and righteousness, and sanctification, and redemption" (1 Corinthians 1:30).

Jesus is made unto us of God's wisdom. He is the true philosophy, the eternal *Sophia,* far above the deepest philosophy—righteousness, sanctification and redemption. So Jesus in our heart becomes our wisdom. He does not improve us and make us something to be wondered at. He just comes in us and lives as He did of old in His Galilean ministry.

When the tabernacle was finished the Holy Spirit came down and possessed it and dwelt in a burning fire upon the ark of the covenant between the cherubim. God lived there after it was dedicated to Him. So when we are dedicated to God, He comes to live in us and transfuses His life through all our being.

He who came into Mary's womb, He who came down in power upon the disciples at Pentecost comes to you and me when we are fully dedicated to Him as real as if we should see Him come fluttering down in visible form upon our shoulder. He comes from heaven to live within us as truly as though we were visibly dwelling under His shadow. God does come to dwell in the heart and live His holy life within us.

In Ezekiel 36 we have this promise: "Then will I sprinkle clean water upon you." That is forgiveness; old sins are all blotted out. "A new heart also will I give you"; that is regeneration. "I will put my spirit within you, and cause you to walk in my statutes, and ye shall keep my judgments, and do *them*." Ah! that is something more than regeneration and forgiveness. It is the living God come to live in the new heart. It is the Holy Spirit dwelling in the heart of flesh that God has given, so that every movement, every thought, every intention, every desire of our whole being will be prompted by the springing life of God within. It is God manifest in the flesh again.

This is the only true consummation of sanctification. Thus only can man enter completely into the life of holiness. As we are possessed by the Holy

Spirit we are made partakers of the divine nature. It is a sacred thing for any man or woman to enter into this relation with God. It places the humblest and most unattractive creature upon the throne with Him. If we know that God is thus dwelling within us, we will bow before the majesty of that sacred presence. We will not dare to profane it by sin. There will be a hush upon our hearts, and we will walk with bowed heads, conscious of the jewel we carry within our hearts.

Do you know what it is to have Christ sanctified to you? Do you know personally what it is to be wholly dedicated to Him and to hear Him say to you, "For your sake I sanctify Myself that you may be truly sanctified"?

HOW SANCTIFICATION IS RECEIVED

1. We must have a divine revelation of our own need of sanctification before we will seek to obtain it. We must see for ourselves that we are not sanctified and that we must be sanctified if we would be happy. The first thing God often does to bring us where we will see this is to make us thoroughly ashamed of ourselves by bringing our frailties to our notice, by letting us fall into mistakes. In these humiliating self-revealings we are able to see where we are not righteous, and we are made to learn that we cannot keep our resolutions of amendment that we make in our own strength. God has let His dear children learn this lesson all through the ages, and learn it by repeated failures. Each of us must learn it for himself.

2. We must come to see Jesus as our Sanctifier. If

with one breath we cry out, "O wretched man that I am! who shall deliver me from the body of this death?" with the next we must add, "I thank God through Jesus Christ my Lord." We must see in Him the great Deliverer and know that He is able to meet our every need and supply it.

3. We must make an entire surrender to Him in everything. We must give ourselves to Him thoroughly, definitely and unconditionally, and have it graven in the heart as if it were written on the rocks or painted on the sky. It must be cut deeply in the annals of our recollection. We must always remember that on that day and on that hour we gave ourselves fully to Christ and He became entirely ours.

4. We must believe that He receives the consecration we make. He is as earnest and as willing and as real about it as we ourselves are. Amid the hush of heaven He stoops to hear our vows and He whispers when we have finished, "It is done. I will give to him of the fountain of the water of life freely. He that overcometh shall inherit all things."

Many people make a mistake about some of these steps. Some of them are clinging to a little of their old goodness and therefore meet with failure. Others stumble at the second step. They do not see that Jesus is their complete Sanctifier. And many cannot take the third step and make a complete surrender of everything to Him. Multitudes fail, even when they have taken these steps, in not being able to believe that Jesus receives them.

Keep these four steps clear: "I am dead, my own life is surrendered and buried out of sight. Jesus is my Sanctifier and my all-in-all. I surrender everything into His hand for Him to do with as He thinks best. I believe He receives the dedication I make to Him and will be in me all I need in this life or in the world to come."

I am certain when you have taken these four steps you can never be as you were before. Something has been done which can never be undone. You have become the Lord's. His presence has come into your heart. It may be like a little trickling spring upon the mountainside, but it will become great rivers of depth and power.

PRACTICAL STEPS

There are certain practical steps by which this life of sanctification is lived out day by day.

1. We are to live a life of implicit obedience to God, doing always what He bids and being wholly under His direction.

2. We are to be obedient to His voice. We will need to listen closely for Jesus speaks softly.

3. In every time of conflict or temptation or testing, we are to draw near to God and give the matter over to Him. Instead of the sweet and happy experiences you would naturally expect after such a consecration, the devil comes and tries to shake your confidence by some trial or temptation. Stand in Him and rejoice that He counts you worthy to receive such trials. If you fail, don't say it is no use to try further. The principle is right. Perhaps you tried to do the work yourself and so you failed. Stop and lay it all at His feet and start afresh, and learn to abide in Him from your very failure.

Israel, after her defeat at Ai, was stronger for

the next conflict. Try to live out the secret you have learned. In human art there is always stumbling at first. You can learn the principles of stenography in a very little while, a few hours perhaps, but it takes months of patient practice to become expert at it.

The moment we are consecrated to Jesus Christ we learn the secret that He is to be all-in-all to us. But when we try to practice this truth, we find that it takes time and patience to learn it thoroughly. We must learn to lean on Him. We must learn little by little how to take Him for every need.

The principle is perfect. It will become absolutely unfailing in practice. Remember the secret is, "Without me ye can do nothing." "I can do all things through Christ which strengtheneth me."

3

Christ Our Healer

Himself took our infirmities, and bare our sicknesses (Matthew 8:17). Jesus Christ the same yesterday, and to day, and for ever (Hebrews 13:8).

Wherever good is to be found, a counterfeit of it will also soon appear. Any valuable coin is always imitated, and the great forger has been at work on divine healing also. It is particularly necessary with this precious truth to guard against error.

WHAT DIVINE HEALING IS NOT

1. Divine healing is not medical healing. It does not come to us through medicines, nor is it God's especial blessing on remedies and means. It is the direct power of the Almighty hand of God himself. "Himself took our infirmities," and He is able to carry them without man's help.

We have nothing to say against the use of remedies so far as those are concerned who are not ready to trust their bodies fully to the Lord. For them it is well enough to use all the help that nature and science can give, and we cheerfully admit that their remedies have some value as far as they go. There is some power in man's attempts to stop the tides of evil that sweep over a suffering world. But there comes a point in all efforts when we have to say, "Thus far shalt thou go and no further."

Yet persons ought not to rashly give up these human helps until they have a better one. Unless they have been led to trust Christ entirely for something higher and stronger than their natural life, they had better stick to natural remedies. They need to be sure that God's Word distinctly presents healing for disease, and does it as definitely as it does for forgiveness of sin.

2. Divine healing is not metaphysical healing. It is not a system of rationalism which is taking on so many forms in the world today, like the chameleon, assuming the hue of the surrounding foliage, according to the class of people it comes in contact with.

What is commonly known as mind cure, or Christian Science, is one of the most familiar forms of metaphysical healing. It places knowledge and intellect, or the mind of man in the place of God. It is not healing by remedies, but by mental force. It is a system of false philosophy and a skeptical theology; a philosophy that is absurd and misleading, and a theology which is atheistic and infidel.

The basis of it is that the material world is not real. What seem to be facts are simply ideas. So the teachers of this error go on to say that there is no body. Disease, therefore, is not real because it has no basis to work on. If you accept this philosophy, the bottom will drop out of all disease. If the idea of sickness has gone from your mind, the trouble has gone. This is a frank, candid statement of the principles of this theory. It has captivated hundreds of thousands of people in this country and hundreds of thousands of dollars have been made out of it.

It is the old philosophy of Hume revived again. The Bible is treated by these teachers in the same way as the body. It is a beautiful system of ideas, but they are only ideas. Genesis is a beautiful story of creation, but it is only an allegory. The New Testament contains a charming picture of Jesus Christ, but it, too, has no foundation in fact. It is the old error that the apostle John wrote strongly against. "Every spirit that confesseth not that Jesus Christ is come in the flesh is not of God: and this is that *spirit* of antichrist, whereof ye have heard that it should come; and even now already is it in the world" (1 John 4:3).

This philosophy denies that Jesus Christ has come in the flesh. It denies the reality of Christ's body; therefore, it is anti-Christian in its teaching. This is *not* divine healing. There is no fellowship between the two. It is one of the delusions of science and would undermine Christianity.

Some of us have despised it so much that perhaps we have not guarded others against it as we should. We have felt it was so silly there could be no harm in it; but we forget how silly human nature is. The apostle tells us the wise in this world are fools with God. "He taketh the wise in their own craftiness" (Job 5:13). How truly this has been fulfilled in the case of New England! That land of colleges, the seat of American intelligence and culture, has given birth to this monstrosity. It is the most fatal infidelity. It does away entirely with the atonement, for where there is no sin there can be no redemption. I would rather be sick all my life with every form of physical torment than be healed by such a lie.

3. Divine healing is not magnetic healing. It is not a mysterious current which flows into one body from another. It is a serious question whether there is such a force in nature as animal magnetism, and whether what this seems to be is not rather an influence to which one person's mind is subject from causes within itself. Whether this is so or not, the thought or claim of such an influence is repudiated by all who act as true ministers of divine healing. Such a one is most anxious to keep his own personality out of the consciousness of the sufferer and hold the eye of the invalid only on Christ, that he may take his healing from Him.

There is nothing to be so much feared in this work as becoming the object of attention. It is heart to heart, and soul to soul contact with the living Christ, and with Him alone, that will accomplish the result.

4. Divine healing is not spiritualism. It cannot be denied that Satan has a certain power over the human body. Certainly he must have if he is able to possess it with disease. And, if he has power to inflict ill health upon the body, I see no reason why he should not, if he please, open the back door and get out and leave the body well. If Satan had power to bind a woman in Christ's time for eighteen years, he had power to unbind her just as quickly. If sickness was his work then,

it must surely be the same now. If he can use some persons better if they are strong and well, he will do so. Other instruments he can use better in weakness and pain.

We cannot but notice the strange persistency with which people of all ages have resorted to evil power, either to appease the evil spirits or enlist their help. The custom is as old as the earliest races. We find it with the Indian in the forest, and the African. These wild incantations have been particularly performed for the healing of sickness, and it is said that many of them have actually resulted in the removal of the disease.

There can be no question that great multitudes of spiritualistic phenomena are real. They give positive evidence of the reality of evil spirits, and they are proofs of God's terrible forewarning, that in the last days the spirits of devils shall be upon the earth working miracles, so that, if possible, they shall deceive the very elect. God's true child will not be deluded by them.

If you are deceived about this thing, look out! You may not be God's true child. I warn you as you value your true welfare, avoid this seductive snare. You will find in it some reality, but it is a dangerous power and it will submerge your Christian faith beneath its hideous waves.

5. Divine healing is not prayer cure. There are many Christians who greatly desire others to pray for them. If they can secure a certain quantity of prayer there will come a corresponding influence for good upon them, and if all the Christians in the world were to pray for them, they would expect to be

healed.

There is a general notion that there is a great deal of power in prayer which must have an effect if it can be concentrated. And if enough of it could be obtained, it would remove mountains and perhaps be able to break down God's stubborn will. This is practically what this view teaches. There is no power in prayer unless it is the prayer of God himself. Unless you are in contact with Christ the living Healer, there is no healing. Christ's healing is by His own divine touch. It is not prayer cure, but Christ the Healer.

6. Divine healing is not faith cure. The term gives a wrong impression, and I am glad it has been discarded. There is danger in getting one's mind so concentrated on faith that it may come between the soul and God. You might as well expect your faith to heal you as to attempt to drink from the handle of the chain pump with which you get fresh water, or to eat the tray upon which your dinner is brought.

If you focus on your faith, you will lose the faith itself. It is God who heals always. The less we dwell on the prayers, the faith or any of the means through which it comes, the more likely we will be to receive the blessing.

7. Divine healing is not will power. No person can grapple with his own helplessness and turn it over into strength. It is a principle of mechanics that no body can move itself. There must be some power outside of itself to do this.

Archimedes said he would be able to pry open the world if he could get some power outside of it to operate on it; but he could not do it from the inside.

If man is down, all the power in his own soul will not avail to lift him up. The trouble too often is in his will. He tries to take hold of himself and lift himself up. He must have some power outside of himself to lift him, or he will remain down.

The will must be yielded up to Christ, and then He will work in us to will and do of His good pleasure. Then the first thought will be—how easy, how delightfully simple it is to receive the power from Him which we need. It is only touching God's hand and receiving strength from His life.

8. Divine healing is not defiance of God's will. It is not saying, "I will have this blessing whether He wills it or not." It is seeing that in having it we have His highest purpose for us. We will not trust for physical healing till we know it is God's will for us, then we can say, "I will it, because He wills it."

9. Neither is divine healing physical immortality, but it is fullness of life until the life-work is done, and then receiving our complete resurrection life at the coming of Christ.

10. Divine healing is not a mercenary medical profession that men adopt as they would adopt a trade or profession in order to make a profit out of it. If you find the mercenary idea appearing in it for a moment, reject and repudiate it. All the gifts of God are as free as the blood of Calvary.

WHAT DIVINE HEALING IS

1. It is the supernatural divine power of God infused into human bodies, renewing their strength and replacing the weakness of suffering human frames by the life and power of God. It is a touch of the divine

Omnipotence, and nothing short of it. It is the same power that raised Jairus's daughter from the dead and that converted your soul.

Is it strange that God should show such power? More power is required to regenerate a lost soul than to raise the dead. God could shiver the sepulcher and bring out the forms of those who have laid there for years with less expenditure of power than it costs Him to redeem one soul and keep His saints steadfast unto the end.

2. It is founded not on the reasoning of man or the testimony of those who have been healed but on the Word of God alone. All the testimony that could be gathered from the whole universe would not establish the truth of such a doctrine, if it is not to be found in the Scriptures. All the deductions of the human intellect are worthless if they are not rooted there. This truth rests on God's eternal Word.

3. It ever recognizes the will of God, and bows to that in profound submission. A Christian who is looking for divine healing will wait till he knows the will of God. Having learned that, he will claim it without wavering.

If a sufferer is convinced that the work God gave him to do is done, and that now he is being called home, then he should acquiesce in that will and lie down in those blessed arms and rest. If that conviction has come to you, I would not dare to shake you out of it, if you have been led into it by God. My only thought would be to sweetly smooth your last pillow, and let you depart in peace.

If, however, you think your work is not done, if you have no clear light from God that this is so, if there is a true and submissive desire in your heart to live and finish your course with joy, then He who said nearly two thousand years ago, "Ought not this woman to be loosed from this bond?" is the same to-day as He was then. He is saying to you in the midst of your weakness, "Should you not be made well?" Surely that should be enough.

It may be, however, that your sickness has been allowed to come as a discipline. You may have been holding back part of the full testimony or service Christ has called you to. I am afraid, then, you cannot be healed until that difficulty is made right. You may be in some wrong and crooked attitude. God probably will not restore you till that is adjusted. He may have called you to some service and you are holding back. There will not be healing for the body till you have yielded at this point.

There are hundreds of meanings in the sicknesses that are allowed to come upon God's dear children, and He will show you what His voice is for you.

For God speaketh once, yea twice, yet man perceiveth it not. In a dream, in a vision of the night, when deep sleep falleth upon men, in slumberings upon the bed; then he openeth the ears of men, and sealeth their instruction, that he may withdraw man from his purpose, and hide pride from man.

He keepeth back his soul from the pit, and his life from perishing by the sword. He is chastened also with pain upon his bed, and the multitude of his bones with strong pain: so that his life abhorreth bread, and his soul dainty meat. His flesh is consumed away, that it cannot be seen; and his bones that were not seen stick out. Yea, his soul draweth near unto the grave, and his life to the destroyers.

If there be a messenger with him, an interpreter, one among a thousand, to shew unto man his uprightness: then he is gracious unto him, and saith, Deliver him from going down to the pit: I have found a ransom. His flesh shall be fresher than a child's: he shall return to the days of his youth (Job 33:14-25).

That is the meaning of many of God's chastenings. There is much that He would say to men through His dealings with their bodies, and it is necessary to get their full meaning into the soul before divine healing can be received, and kept after it has been received. It is not a cast-iron patent that works inexorably in one way always. It requires a very close walk with God. When the soul is walking in harmony and obedience to Him, the life of God can fully flow into the body. Thank God we cannot have it and have the devil, too.

3. Divine healing is part of the redemption work of Jesus Christ. It is one of the things He came to bring. Its foundation stone is the cross of Calvary. He "redeemeth thy life from destruction." "Deliver him from going down to the pit: I have found a ran-. som." Surely that healing comes from Himself alone. "By whose stripes ye were healed." That is the redemption work of Christ. You have a right to it, for His body bore all the liability of your body on the cross. Take it and love Him better, because it came from His stripes.

I love to think of that word in the singular, stripe. That is the Greek meaning. His body was so beaten that it was all one stripe. Every inch of His flesh was lacerated for us. Christ suffered to redeem every fiber of our body.

4. Divine healing comes to us through the life of Jesus Christ who rose from the dead in His own body. He has gone up to heaven with His living body. You can see Him there today, with hands and feet of living flesh and bones which you can touch. He can sit with you today at the table and eat as He did of old.

He is no shadowy, cloudlike form, but He has flesh and bones as we have. That is our Christ, a living physical Christ, and He is able and willing to share His physical life with you, by breathing His strength into you. We are healed by the life of Christ in our body. It is a tender union with Him; nearer than the bond of marriage; so near that the very life of His veins is transfused into ours. That is divine healing.

5. It is the work of the Holy Spirit, quickening the body. When Christ healed the sick while He was upon earth, it was not by the Deity that dwelt in His humanity. He said, "If I cast out devils by the Spirit of God, then the kingdom of God is come unto you" (Matthew 12:28). Jesus healed by the Holy Spirit. "The Spirit of the Lord *is* upon me, because he hath anointed me to preach the gospel to the poor; he hath sent me to heal the brokenhearted" (Luke 4:18). The Holy Spirit is the agent, then, by which this great power is wrought.

We should especially expect to see His working in these days because they are the days of His own dispensation, the days in which it has been prophesied that there shall be signs and wonders. How did Samson receive his strength? When the Spirit of the Lord came upon him. Then he was able to hurl the temple into ruins and their god Dagon with it. The Spirit of

God was in his flesh. So when this electric fire is running through our frame, it brings healing and strength to every fiber.

6. Divine healing comes by the grace of God, not through the work of man. It cannot be bought; neither can it be worked for. We cannot help God out in it. We must take it as a gift. It comes to us as pardon does, a free gift from Him.

7. Divine healing comes to us by faith. It is not the faith that heals; God heals, but faith enables us to receive it. We must believe that God is healing before any evidence is given. It is to be believed as a present reality and then ventured on. We are to act as if it were already true. God wants us to lean on Him, and trust Him, and then rejoice and praise Him for what He has given, with no doubt or fear.

8. Divine healing is in accordance with all the facts of church history. From the time of Irenaeus down to the present century there have been repeated examples of it. It is a long array, and great multitudes of healed ones proclaim with one voice: "Jesus Christ, the same yesterday, and to day, and for ever."

All down through the middle ages the pure Church believed this truth and taught it. The Waldenses held it as an article of their faith. The times of the early reformers are full of it. The lives of Luther and Baxter, of Fox and Whitfield, and of John Wesley give clear and convincing testimony that they believed this truth.

In later times the examples of it are numerous. Germany, Switzerland, Sweden, Norway, England and her colonies, and the mission fields of the world, have many witnesses to the healing power of Jesus.

Our own land is full of it. We have many witnesses to it in our midst. We know them, and how some of them have stood the test of publicity and of years. They are not obscure cases. Many of them are men and women who have stood in the very front of Christian work. There is every kind of character and intelligence and temperament and disposition among them. There are children among them, as well as old men. Some of them have had lofty intellects, but they have been transformed into simple children. There are all classes of disease among them—from the terrible cancer to the most disordered of nervous organisms. And He has healed them all.

9. Divine healing is one of the signs of the age. It is the forerunner of Christ's coming. It is God's answer to the infidelity of today. Man may try to reason it down with the force of his intellect. God meets it with this unanswerable proof of His power.

HOW IS JESUS OUR HEALER?

1. He has bought healing for us with His stripes. It is a part of His purchased redemption on Calvary. "Surely he hath borne our griefs and carried our sorrows" (Isaiah 53:4).

2. Healing is in His risen life, which is in us. We have healing not only *from* Jesus, but *in* Jesus. It is in His living body, and we receive it as we abide in Him and keep it only as we abide in Him.

3. He enables us to receive healing by becoming our power to believe. He gives the faith to trust Him if we will receive it. We do not have to climb heights to find Him, but He comes down to our helplessness and becomes our trust as well as our healing.

A Chinese was once telling the difference between Christ and Confucius and Buddha. He said:

"I was down in a deep pit, half sunk in the mire and was crying for someone to help me out. As I looked up I saw a venerable, gray-haired man looking down at me. His countenance bore the marks of his pure and holy spirit. 'My son,' he said, 'this is a dreadful place.' 'Yes,' I said, 'I fell into it. Can't you help me out?' 'My son,' he said, 'I am Confucius. If you had read my books and followed what they taught, you never would have been here.' 'Yes, father,' I said, 'but can't you help me out?' As I looked up he was gone.

"Soon I saw another form approaching, and another man bent over me, this time with closed eyes and folded arms. He seemed to be looking into some far-off, distant place. 'My son,' he said, 'just close your eyes and fold your arms and forget all about yourself. Get into a state of perfect rest. Don't think about anything that could disturb. Get so still that nothing can move you. Then, my child, you will be in such delicious rest as I am.' 'Yes, father,' I answered, 'I'll do that when I am above ground. Can't you help me out?' But Buddha, too, was gone.

"I was just beginning to sink into despair when I saw another Figure above me, different from the others. He was very simple, and looked just like the rest of us, but there were the marks of suffering in His face. I cried out to Him: 'Oh, Father, can you help me?' 'My child,' He said, 'what is the matter?' Before I could answer Him, He was down in the mire by my side; He folded His arms about me and lifted me up, and then He fed and rested me. When I was well, He did not say, 'Now, don't do that again,' but He said, 'We will walk on together now'; and we have been walking together until this day."

That's what Jesus Christ will do for you! He comes down to you where you are. He becomes your trust within you, and then you go on together until the resurrection light and glory of the coming age bursts in upon you.

May God help us all to receive Him fully for His own name's sake! Amen.

4

Christ Our Coming Lord

I will give him the morning star (Revelation 2:28).

The second coming of the Lord Jesus Christ is a distinct and important part of the apostolic gospel. "I declare unto you the gospel," Paul says to the Corinthians, and then begins to tell them of the resurrection and the second advent. It is, indeed, good news to all who love Him and mourn the sins and sorrows of a ruined world.

It is the glorious culmination of all other parts of the gospel. We have spoken of the gospel of *salvation*, but Peter says our salvation is "ready to be revealed in the last time." Then only, when we stand amid the wrecks of time and secure upon the Rock of Ages,

> *Then, Lord, shall I fully know,*
> *Not till then, how much I owe.*

(53)

We have spoken of *sanctification,* but John says: "When he shall appear, we shall be like him . . . and every man that hath this hope in him purifieth himself, even as he is pure" (1 John 3:2-3). And we have spoken of *divine healing,* but Paul says: "God hath given us the earnest of the resurrection in our bodies now," and divine healing is but the first-springing life of which the resurrection will be the full fruition.

The truth and hope of the Lord's coming is linked with all truth and life. It is the Church's great and blessed hope. In the very beginning of human history God placed this great hope before His children. In the hour when man fell from Paradise, God erected in that fallen Eden in the majestic figures of the cherubim, the prophecy and symbol of man's future glory. The faces of the lion, the ox, the man and the eagle were the types of royalty, the strength, the wisdom and the lofty elevation to which redeemed man was to rise in Jesus.

These figures run through all the dispensations. They are God's portrait of His redeemed child after redemption's work is done. God sets before Himself and before man His sublime ideal for his future, and He will never rest till it is fulfilled. It is, therefore, well that besides the gospel for the present, we should understand, and live under the power of the gospel of the future and the blessed and purifying hope of Christ's glorious coming.

WHAT WE MEAN BY CHRIST'S COMING

1. We do not mean His coming to the individual Christian's heart. He does thus come most truly and graciously, and this is the blessed mystery of which

we have already spoken in connection with our sanctification. It is "Christ in you, the hope of glory." But this is not His second coming.

Some persons are ready to say, with a great show of spirituality, I have the millennium in my heart, and the Lord in my heart; let those who have not, speculate about a material coming. Well, Paul had the Lord in his heart, and a millennium as near to the third heaven as these persons will probably claim. John was about as near his Redeemer's heart as any of us can ever expect to get on earth. But they did speak and write in terms like this: "Then we which are alive and remain unto the coming of the Lord . . . shall be caught up together with them in the clouds, to meet the Lord in the air." "We know that when He shall appear, we shall appear with Him in glory." "Behold, he cometh with clouds; and every eye shall see him" (Revelation 1:7). Even so, come, Lord Jesus.

Indeed, the more we know Jesus spiritually, the more will we long for His personal and eternal presence in the fuller and more glorious sense which His personal advent will bring.

2. We do not mean His coming at death. It is doubtful whether He does really come for us at death. Lazarus is represented as borne by angels into Abraham's bosom; and Stephen at his glorious departing saw Jesus in heaven on the right hand of God, rising, it is true, to receive and honor His faithful servant but not coming for him personally.

The contrasts between death and the Lord's coming are very marked. We are not told to watch for death, but are delivered from its fear. We are to watch for the Lord's coming. Death is an enemy; His coming a welcome visitation of our dearest friend. Death is a bitter bereavement to the heart; the Lord's coming is the very consolation of the bereaved, and the antidote of death.

If death and the Lord's coming were identical, then the apostle would have said to the Thessalonian believers: "I would not have you ignorant concerning them that are asleep, that ye sorrow not as those that have no hope, for the Lord has come for them, and will soon in like manner come for you in death, and you shall be sweetly united in death once more." Does he say that? No! But he does say: "The Lord himself shall descend from heaven . . . and the dead in Christ shall rise first: then we which are alive and remain shall be caught up together with them in the clouds to meet the Lord in the air: and so shall we ever be with the Lord" (1 Thessalonians 4:16-17).

It is not death he points them to, but that which is to overcome death, and of which he says in writing to the Corinthians: "Then shall be brought to pass the saying that is written, 'Death is swallowed up in victory'." If the Lord's coming is to swallow up death in victory, it is very certain that it cannot be the same thing, or it would swallow up itself.

3. We do not mean the spiritual coming of Christ through the spread of the gospel and the progress of Christianity. This is nowhere recognized in the Bible as the personal coming of Christ.

"Behold, he cometh with clouds; and every eye shall see him, and they also which pierced him: and all kindreds of the earth shall wail because of him" (Revelation 1:7). Now, that is not the way they do when they receive the gospel. They rejoice. But now they are startled and discouraged. And they cry, as represented in another place, to the rocks and the mountains to fall upon them and hide them from the wrath of the Lamb.

So, also, the angels, speaking of this event to the eleven disciples, say: "This same Jesus shall so come in like manner as ye have seen him go into heaven." This cannot be the publication of the gospel, but must be His personal, visible and glorious appearing. The gospel is to be widely diffused; His truth is to prevail; His cause is to triumph. But He is coming personally, and He is infinitely more than even His truth and cause.

WHAT DO WE MEAN BY THE MILLENNIUM?

Some persons have stated that the doctrine of the millennium is a modern invention, and that the word itself is not found in the Bible.

The word millennium is not English but is the Greek word for *a thousand years*. It is used repeatedly in Revelation 20 to denote the period during which Christ shall reign with His saints on the earth after the first resurrection. It is a time of victory, joy and glory. Seven special facts are recorded concerning it here:

1. The resurrection and reunion of the saints
2. Their reward and reign
3. The complete exclusion of Satan from the earth
4. The personal and continual presence of Jesus with them on earth
5. The suppression of all enemies and the universal reign of righteousness

6. The duration of a thousand years

7. The immediately succeeding revolt of Satan and sinful man and the final judgment of the wicked

If there was no other reference in the Bible to this time of blessing, these elements alone would be sufficient to constitute a state and time of exalted glory and happiness. Much more do they suffice to identify it as the golden age of which former prophets wrote and spoke, when righteousness, truth and peace shall "cover the earth as the waters cover the sea."

THE ORDER OF THESE TWO EVENTS

The order of Christ's coming and the millennium is the next question to be settled, and upon it hang most of the issues of the question. Is the coming of Christ to precede or follow this millennial period?

1. The most obvious reason for believing that it precedes it is found in the very passage just referred to where these events are both described. There can be no question that here the coming of the Lord precedes and introduces the millennium. His coming is minutely depicted in the whole procession from heaven to earth. Then follows the conquest and punishment of His earthly foes, the binding of Satan, the resurrection of the saints, the reign of the risen ones and the thousand years.

The only way it is attempted to set this aside is to represent it as figurative and spiritual. Dean Alford's strong sense and honesty is the best answer to this. If this be so, he declares, then adieu to all definiteness and certainty in the Scriptures. If this be not a literal coming, resurrection and millennium, then we do not know what our Bibles mean.

2. The next argument for Christ's premillennial coming is the emphatic use of the word *watch* in connection with it. Many times we are told to watch for it. Now if it is to be preceded by a spiritual millennium, the Lord would have told us to watch for this. How could the early Church watch for His coming, how can even we if we know that it is to be preceded by a clear thousand years? The very word *watch* means imminency, and Christ's return is not imminent if ten whole centuries must intervene.

If it be objected that as a matter of fact Christ's coming did not occur during more than ten centuries, this does not alter its imminency. An event may be liable to occur at any moment for years, and yet be long retarded. That is quite different from its being understood as not to occur until the later period. Although God knows just the moment when His Son will appear, He wants His Church to be always expecting it—at evening or at midnight or at the cock crowing or in the morning.

The announcement of a fixed previous millennium would have been fatal to this design, and the Church would have gone to work to make her own millennium without Him. This is just what the Roman Catholic Church did, when Pope Hildebrand announced in the tenth century that the millennium had begun and that Christ was already present through His vicar. And some Protestant teachers have the assumption to tell us today that this century of progress is the first age of the millennium.

3. The next proof of a premillennial coming is found in the picture Christ gives us of the condition of things as they were to be down to the close of the

Christian age, and up to the very hour of His coming. Just glance at a few bold touches in the picture.

• Some seed fell by the wayside and the fowls of the air devoured them; some fell on stony places and perished; some were choked by thorns, and some fell on good ground and bore fruit.

The enemy sowed the tares, and both the good seed and the tares grow together till the harvest.

• The Church, externally, grows up into luxuriant strength like the mustard plant, but internally is full of leaven.

• The true and pure are like the hid treasure and the pearl, so hard to find.

• The net gathers of every kind and only the angels can separate the evil at the last.

As the ages roll on, there looms up the picture, not of a millennium, but a "falling away first." "Wickedness shall abound and the love of many shall wax cold." "Many shall depart from the faith, giving heed to doctrines of devils." "In the last days perilous times shall come." There shall be plenty of church members "having a form of godliness"; but these shall be the very enemies of the Cross of Christ, "denying the power thereof."

A holy, happy world will not be waiting to welcome its King, but "as a snare shall He come unto all that dwell on the earth." "When they shall say, 'Peace and safety,' then sudden destruction." And when it bursts upon them, it shall find them "as it was in the days of Noah and of Lot"; and the Master even asks, "When the Son of man cometh, shall He find faith on the earth?"

This is God's picture of the future of earth until

Christ's coming. It does not look much like a previous millennium.

No, nor does the story of eighteen centuries move toward a spiritual millennium. If this be the best God has for us, then prophecy is an exaggeration and the Bible a poetic dream. Thank God, He is coming and His Kingdom shall transcend our brightest hope and His own most glowing picture.

OBJECTIONS

The strongest objections made to this doctrine of Christ's second coming are these:

1. It dishonors the work of the Holy Spirit, as if He were incompetent to fulfill His administration and were represented as having failed in His great mission to convert the world, so that some other means had to be provided. In reply it is enough to say that the Holy Spirit has not undertaken to convert the world, but to call out of it the Church of Christ and prepare a people for His name.

When this is done, and all who will accept Jesus as a Savior have been called, converted and fully trained, the time for the next stage will have come. Jesus will come to reign and restore His ancient people for their privileges and opportunities. The work of the Holy Spirit will not cease then, for He shall abide with us forever, and the ages to come shall afford unbounded and more glorious scope for His grace and power.

2. It is objected that such a doctrine discourages Christian missions, and saps the foundations of the Church's most glorious hopes and prospects. On the contrary, it opens a prospect of far grander glory to

the Church at her Lord's appearing, and bids her go
forth, rapt with the desire to hasten it, to prepare the
world for His appearing. As an incentive to this
work, He himself has told her that when the message
of salvation has been proclaimed to all the world,
then shall the end come.

The fact is that a large majority of the missionaries
now in foreign lands believe and rejoice in the
blessed hope of the Lord's coming, and are animated
by it to labor for the world's evangelization. They
are cheered by the blessed thought that their task is
not to convert the whole human race but to evangelize the nations and give every man a chance to be
saved if he will. They would, indeed, be distracted
and dismayed at the prospect they behold, did they
feel that the world must wait until the present agen-
cies have wrought out its full salvation, while mean-
while three times its entire population every century
is swept into eternity unsaved.

The coming of Christ is not going to suspend
mission work. It will bring the most glorious and
complete system of evangelization earth has ever
seen. And under its benign influence the heathen
shall all be brought to Jesus; all nations shall be
blessed in Him, and all people shall call Him blessed.
The most ardent friends of lost humanity must long
the most for this, the world's best hope.

3. It is objected that this doctrine leads to fanaticism. Anything may be abused, but in the sober and
scriptural faith of this doctrine there is nothing
fitted to minister to rashness, presumption or folly.
Let us very carefully avoid all attempts to prophesy
ourselves, or to be wise above that which is written.

But let us not be intimidated by the devil's howl from the fullness of God's truth and testimony.

This truth will make us a peculiar people. It will take away the charm of the world, and separate us from it. It will make us very unlike many selfish and comfortable Christians and will set our soul on fire to serve God and save men. And if that be fanaticism, then welcome such fanaticism.

4. The premillennial doctrine is objected to as gross and material, tending to promote earthly and carnal hopes in the heart and the Church, like the earthly ideas and ambitions of the primitive apostles which the Master rebuked. He taught them to look for a spiritual kingdom and a heavenly home. That was the extreme then, may not the opposite be now? Is not the true need the spiritual first, afterward the material; the resurrection life of the soul first, then the resurrection of the body?

We do not hold or teach any gross or material idea of the millennial age. The bodies of the saints will be spiritual and like His own. But if He was pleased to take such a body into the heavenly world and make it the center and crown of creation, is it anything but an affectation to try to be more spiritual than our Lord? Nay, it is all spiritual, and the true purpose and end of redemption is that "our whole spirit and soul and body be preserved blameless unto the coming of our Lord Jesus Christ," and "the whole *earth* be filled with His glory."

THE SIGNS OF HIS COMING

While the day and the hour shall be unrevealed, yet His children "are not in darkness that that day should overtake them as a thief." As the end approaches, "none of the wicked shall understand, but the wise shall understand."

There is a distinct order revealed. He will first come for His own waiting ones, and they, with the holy dead, shall be caught up to meet Him in the air. The wicked world shall be left behind; a formal church and a multitude of nations shall live on and scarcely miss the little flock that has just been caught away. Then will begin a series of judgments and warnings, ending at last in the descent of Christ in power and glory, the revelation of His righteous judgment against His open enemies and the beginning of His personal reign.

There will thus be two appearings of Jesus Christ—the one to His own, the other, later, to the entire world; the first as a Bridegroom, the second as a King and Judge. The signs of the one do not therefore apply to the other. The first of these appearings is not so sharply defined as the other. It is more imminent and uncertain, and may come at any hour.

Many of the most important signs of the Lord's coming have already been fulfilled. For example:

1. The political changes and developments of Daniel's great visions have apparently all occurred. The great empires have come and gone, and the minor kingdoms which were to succeed them are now covering the regions which once they swayed.

2. The Jewish signs have not been less remarkable. Jacob is turning his face again to Bethel, and Jerusalem is putting on her beautiful garments again. Her sons are slowly gathering, while jealous nations are

hastening the exodus, and fulfilling unconsciously the voice of prophecy.

3. The intellectual signs are not less marked. Knowledge is indeed increased, and many run to and fro, while human philosophy talks of evolution and declares that all things continue as they were and nature is immutable and only material.

4. The moral signs are even more marked than Daniel's picture. The predicted "falling away" has long ago begun. "The wicked shall do wickedly" was never more true than today. Portentous forms of wickedness startle the moral sense every day, and invention is as ripe in evil as it is in material art.

5. The religious signs are growing more vivid. Lukewarmness and wordliness in the church, intense longings after holiness on the part of the few, and a mighty missionary movement are the features of the age, and the signs of prophecy, that point to the day of the Son of Man.

6. And finally, an earnest, a growing and a world-wide expectation of His coming on the part of all those who love His appearing is as profound today as it was in Judea, and even the Gentile world in the age preceding His advent at Bethlehem. The morning star is in the East. "The children of the day" have seen it. The cry has gone forth, "The night is far spent, the day is at hand." Soon the Sun will fill the sky and cover the earth with millennial glory.

THE BLESSINGS OF HIS COMING

1. Christ's return will bring us Jesus himself. This is the best of its blessings. Like all the other sections

of this gospel, this, too, is the gospel of Himself. Not the robes and the royal crowns, not the resurrection bodies or reunited friends will be the chief joys, but

> *Thou art coming, we shall see Thee,*
> *And be like Thee on that day.*

2. It will bring us our friends. "Them who sleep in Jesus will God bring with Him." They shall be alive, they shall be recognized, they shall be gloriously beautiful, they shall be ours forever. Not only the old ones, but such new ones, the good of all the ages, the men and women we have longed to know. What a family!

> *Ten thousand times ten thousand*
> *In sparkling raiment bright,*
> *The armies of the ransomed saints*
> *Throng up the steeps of light.*

> . . . .

> *Oh, then what raptured greetings*
> *On Canaan's happy shore;*
> *What knitting severed friendships up*
> *Where partings are no more.*

3. Jesus' coming will bring us perfect spirits, restored to His image, glorious in His likeness, free from fault, defect, or imperfection, removed above temptation, incapable of falling and overflowing with unutterable blessedness. We shall wear His perfect image; we shall know as we are known; we shall be as holy as He is holy; we shall possess His strength and beauty and perfect love. The universe will gaze upon us, and next to the glory of the Lamb will be the

beauty of the bride.

4. We shall have perfect bodies; we shall possess His perfect resurrection life; we shall forget even what a pain was like; we shall spring into boundless strength; our hearts shall thrill with the fullness of immortal life; space and distance shall be annihilated. The laws of gravitation will hold us no more. The New Jerusalem in length and breadth and height is the same. Our bodies shall be the perfect instruments of our exalted spirits, the exact reflection of His glorious body.

5. Christ's coming will give us the sweetest and highest service. It will be no idle, selfish ecstasy, but it will bring a perfect partnership in His kingdom and administration. We shall, perhaps, be permitted to fulfill the ideals of our highest earthly experiences, and finish the work we have longed and tried to do—with boundless resources, infinite capabilities, unlimited scope and time, and His own presence and omnipotent help. The blessed work will be to serve Him, to bless others, and to raise earth and humanity to happiness, righteousness and Paradise restored.

6. His coming will banish Satan. It will bind and chain the foe and fiend, whose hate and power have held the world in ages of darkness and misery. Oh, to be free from his presence for even a day! Oh, to feel that we need no longer watch with ceaseless vigilance against him! Oh, to walk upon a world without a devil! Lord, hasten that glorious day!

7. And it will bring such blessings to others, to the race, to the world. It will stop the awful tragedy of sin and suffering; it will sheathe the sword, emanci-

pate the captive, close the prison and the hospital, bind the devil and his henchman, Death. It will beautify and glorify the face of the earth, evangelize and convert the perishing nations, shed light and gladness on this dark scene of woe and wickedness.

There shall be no more crying,
  There shall be no more pain,
There shall be no more dying,
  There shall be no more stain.

Hearts that by death were riven
  Meet in eternal love;
Lives on the altar given
  Rise to their crowns above.

Satan shall tempt us never,
  Sin shall o'ercome no more,
Joy shall abide for ever,
  Sorrow and grief be o'er.

Hasten, sweet morn of gladness,
  Hasten, dear Lord, we pray;
Finish this night of sadness,
  Hasten the heavenly day.

Jesus, our watch we are keeping,
  Longing for Thee to come;
Then shall be ended our night of weeping,
  Then we shall reach our home.

(A.B. Simpson, "No More Sorrow")

THE LESSONS HIS COMING LEAVES

1. Let us be ready. "The marriage of the Lamb is

come, and his wife hath made herself ready. And to her was granted that she should be arrayed in fine linen, clean and white" (Revelation 19:7-8). Thank God that the robes are *given*. Let us have them on. *White robes*. When the Bride is dressed, the wedding must be near. So let us hasten His coming.

2. Let us be watching. "Behold, I come as a thief. Blessed is he that watcheth, and keepeth his garments, lest he walk naked, and they see his shame" (Revelation 16:15). Let us not put off the wedding robe for an hour. Let us remember His words: "When these things begin to come to pass, then look up, and lift up your heads; for your redemption draweth nigh" (Luke 21:28). Keep your faces turned heavenward until your whole being shall curve heavenward.

3. Be faithful. His coming brings the reward of faithful servants. "Look to yourselves, that we lose not those things which we have wrought, but that we receive a full reward." "Hold that fast which thou hast, that no man take thy crown."

In the ancient church there was a noble band of forty faithful soldiers in one of the Roman legions who were condemned to die for their faith in Jesus. They were all exposed on the center of a frozen lake, to perish on the ice, but allowed the choice of recanting from their faith at any moment during the fatal night by walking to the shore and reporting to the officer on duty.

As the night wore on the sentinel on shore saw a cloud of angels hovering over the place where the martyrs stood, and as one by one they dropped, they placed a crown upon the martyr's brow and bore him up to the skies, while all the air rang with the song, "Forty Martyrs and Forty Crowns."

At last they had all gone but one, and his crown still hung in the sky above and no one seemed to claim it. Suddenly the sentinel heard a step, and lo! one of the forty was at his side. He had fled. The sentinel looked at him as he took down his name, and then said: "Fool, had you seen what I have seen this night you would not have lost your crown. But it shall not be lost. Take my place, and I will gladly take yours"; and forth he marched to death and glory, while again the silent choir took up the chorus, "Forty Martyrs and Forty Crowns. Thou hast been faithful unto death and thou shalt receive a crown of life."

God help us to hear that chorus when He shall come!

4. Be diligent. There is much to do. You can "hasten the coming of the day of God." The world is to be forewarned. The Church is to be prepared. Arouse thee, O Christian. Give Him every power, every faculty, every dollar, every moment. Send the gospel abroad. Go yourself if you can. If you cannot, send your substitute. And may this present time mean for you and for this world—as nothing ever meant before—a time of preparation for the coming of our Lord and Savior Jesus Christ!

5

The Walk
with God

*He that saith he abideth in him ought himself
also so to walk, even as he walked (1 John 2:6).*

The life naturally leads to the walk. The term
describes the course of life, the conduct, the
practical side of our Christian life. The reference to
the walk of our Lord Jesus Christ recalls His character and life. The character of Jesus stands out as the
divinest monument of the Bible and the Gospels.

Even men who do not believe in Him as we do
have been compelled to acknowledge the grandeur
and loftiness of His incomparable life. Renan said,
"The Christ of the Gospels is the most beautiful
Incarnation of God. His beauty is eternal; His reign
shall never end." Goethe said, "There shines from
the Gospels a sublimity through the person of Christ
which only the divine could manifest."

Rosseau wrote: "Was He no more than man?
What sweetness! What purity in His ways! What
tender grace in His teaching! What loftiness in His

maxims! What wisdom in His words! What delicacy in His touch! What an empire in the hearts of His followers! Where is the man, where is the sage that could suffer and die without weakness or display? So grand, so inimitable is His character that the inventors of such a story would be more wonderful than the character which they portrayed."

Carlyle said, "Jesus Christ is the divinest Symbol. Higher than this human thought can never go." Napoleon said, "I am a man; I understand men. . . . Jesus Christ was more than man. Our empire is built on force, His on love, and it will last when ours has passed away."

But if Jesus Christ thus appears at a distance to the minds that can only admire Him, how much more must He be to those who know Him as a personal Friend and who see Him in the light of love, for

> The love of Jesus, what it is,
> None but His loved ones know.

The character and life of Christ have a completeness of detail which no other Bible biography possesses. The story has been written out by many witnesses, and the portrait is reproduced in all its lineaments and features. He has traversed every stage of life from the cradle to the grave, and represented humanity in every condition and circumstance of temptation, trial and need, so that His example is equally suited to childhood, youth or manhood. It is suited to the humble and the poor in life's lowliest path or to the sovereign who sways the widest scepter, for Jesus is at once the lowly Nazarene and the Lord of lords.

Christ has felt the throb of every human affection. He has felt the pang of every human sorrow. He is the Son of Man in the largest, broadest sense. Nay, His humanity is so complete that He represents the softer traits of womanhood as well as the virility and strength of manhood and even the simplicity of a little child. There is no place in the experiences of life where we may not look back at this Pattern Life for light and help as we bring it into touch with our need and ask, "What would Jesus do?"

God has sent forth the life of Christ as our example and commanded us to imitate and reproduce Him in our lives. This is not an ideal picture to study as we would some paragon of art. It is a life to be lived and it is adapted to all the needs of our present existence. It is a plain life for a common people to copy, a type of humanity that we can take with us into the kitchen and the family room, into the workshop and the place of business, into the field where the farmer toils, and the orchard where the gardener prunes. We can take Him into the place where the tempter assails and even the lot where want and poverty press us with their burdens and their cares. This Christ is the Christ of every man who will receive Him as a Brother and follow Him as an Example and a Master. "I have given you an example," He says, "that ye should do as I have done."

Jesus expects us to be like Him. Are we copying Him and being made conformable into His image? There is but one Pattern. For ages God "sought for a man and found none." At last humanity produced a perfect type, and since then God has been occupied in making other men according to this Pattern. He is the one original. When Judson came to America the religious papers were comparing him to Paul and the early apostles, and Judson wrote expressing his grief and displeasure, saying, "I do not want to be like them. There is but One to copy: Jesus himself. I want to plant my feet in His footprints. . . . He is the only Copy. I want to be like Him." So let us seek to walk even as He walked.

The secret of a Christlike life lies partly in the deep longing for it. We grow like the ideals that we admire. We reach unconsciously at last the things we aspire to. Ask God to give you a high conception of the character of Christ and an intense desire to be like Him and you will never rest until you reach your ideal.

THE MOTIVE OF JESUS' LIFE

The key to any character is to be found in its supreme motive, the great end which it is pursuing, the object for which it is living. We cannot understand conduct by merely looking at facts. We need to grasp the intent that lies behind these facts and incidents, and the supreme reason that controls these actions. When a great crime has been committed, the object of the detective is to establish a reason for it; then everything else can be made plain. The great object for which we are living will determine everything else, and explain many things which otherwise might seem inexplicable.

When the ploughman starts out to make a straight furrow he needs two stakes. The nearer stake is not enough. He must keep it in line with the farther one, the stake at the remotest end of the ridge, and as he keeps the two in line his course is straight. It is the final goal which determines our immediate actions and if that is high enough, and strong enough, it will attract us like a heavenly magnet from all lesser and lower things, and hold us irresistibly to our heavenly pathway.

The supreme motive of Christ's life was devotion to the will and glory of God. "Wist ye not that I must be about my Father's business?" This was the deep conviction even upon the heart of the child (Luke 2: 49). "My meat is to do the will of him that sent me" (John 4:34). "I seek not mine own will, but the will of the Father that sent me" (John 5:30). "I came down from heaven, not to do mine own will, but the will of him that sent me" (John 6:38). This was the purpose of His adult life.

"I have glorified thee on the earth: I have finished the work which thou gavest me to do" (John 17:4). This was His joyful cry as He finished His course and handed back His commission to the Father who sent Him. Is this the supreme object of our life, and are we pressing on to it through good report and evil report, caring only to please our Master and have His approval in the end?

THE PRINCIPLE OF HIS LIFE

Every life can be summed up in some controlling principle. With some it is selfishness in the various forms of avarice, ambition or pleasure. With others it is devotion to some favorite pursuit of art or literature or invention and discovery. With Jesus Christ the one principle of His life was love, and the law that He has left for us is the same simple and comprehensive law of love. It includes every form of duty in the one new commandment: "A new commandment I give unto you, That ye love one another; as I have loved you" (John 13:34).

This is not the Old Testament law of love with self in the center: "Thou shalt love thy neighbor as thyself." This is a new commandment with Christ in the center: "That ye love one another, as I have loved you" (John 15:12). Love for His Father, love for His own, love for the sinful, love for His enemies—this covered the whole life of Jesus Christ and this will comprehend the length and breadth of the life of His followers. This will simplify every question, solve every problem and sweeten every duty into a delight. It will make our life as His was, an embodiment of that beautiful ideal which the Holy Spirit has left us in the thirteenth chapter of First Corinthians: "Love is patient, love is kind, and is not jealous; love does not brag and is not arrogant, does not act unbecomingly; it does not seek its own, is not provoked, does not take into account a wrong suffered, does not rejoice in unrighteousness, but rejoices with the truth; bears all things, believes all things, hopes all things, endures all things" (vv. 4-7, NASB).

THE RULE AND STANDARD OF HIS LIFE

Every life must have a standard by which it is regulated, and so Christ's life was molded by the Holy Scriptures. "These are the words which I spake unto you, while I was yet with you, that all things must be fulfilled, which were written in the law of Moses, and in the prophets, and in the psalms, concerning me" (Luke 24:44).

It was necessary that Christ's life should fulfill the Scriptures. He could not die upon the cross until He had first lived out every word that had been written concerning Him. It is just as necessary that our lives should fulfill the Scriptures; we have no right to let a single promise or command in His holy Book be a dead letter insofar as we are concerned. God wants us while we live to prove in our own experience all things that have been written in the Bible and to bind the Bible in a new and living edition of flesh and blood in our own lives.

THE SOURCE OF HIS LIFE

Where did Jesus derive the strength for this supernatural and perfect example? Was it through His own inherent and essential deity? Or did He suspend during the days of His humiliation His own self-contained rights and powers and live among us simply as a man, dependent for His support upon the same sources of strength that we enjoy? It would seem so. Listen to His own confession: "The Son can do nothing of himself, but what he seeth the Father do. I can of mine own self do nothing: as I hear, I judge. As the living Father hath sent me, and I live by the Father: so he that eateth me, even he shall live by me" (John 5:19, 30; 6:57).

This seems to make it very plain that our Lord derived His daily strength from the same source as we may receive ours: by communion with God, by a life of dependence, faith and prayer, and by receiving and being ever filled with the presence and power of the Holy Spirit.

If we would therefore walk as He walked, let us receive the Holy Spirit as He did at His baptism. Let us constantly depend upon Him and be filled with His presence. Let us live a life of unceasing prayer. Let us draw our strength each moment from Him as He did from the Father. Let our life for both soul and body be sustained by the inbreathing of His so that it shall be true of us: "In him we live, and move, and have our being" (Acts 17:28).

This was the Master's life and this may be ours. What an inspiration it is for us to know that He humbled Himself to the same place of dependence in which we stand, and that He will exalt us through His grace to the same victories which He won.

THE ACTIVITIES OF HIS LIFE

The life of Jesus Christ was a positive one. It was not all absorbed in self-contemplation and self-culture, but it went out in thoughtful benevolence to the world around Him. His brief biography as given by Peter is one of practical and holy activity. "He went about doing good" (Acts 10:38). In His three-and-a-half-year ministry, He travelled on foot over every portion of Galilee, Samaria and Judea, incessantly preaching, teaching and working with arduous toil. He was constantly thronged by the multitudes so that Luke tells us "there was not time so much as to eat." Once at the close of a busy day He was so weary that He fell asleep on the little ship amid the raging storm. When He left His busy toil for a season of rest the multitudes still pressed upon Him, and He could not be silent. After a Sabbath of continuous labor at Capernaum we find Him rising the next morning a great while before day that He might steal from His slumber the time to pray.

His life was one of ceaseless service, and even still on His ascension throne He is continually employed in ministries of active love. So He has said to us that we must copy Him. No consecrated Christian can be an idler or a drone. "As my Father hath sent me even so send I you." We are here as missionaries, every one of us with a commission and a trust just as definite as those whom we send overseas. Let us find our work, and, like Him, "whatsoever thy hand findeth to do, do it with thy might" (Ecclesiastes 9: 10).

SEPARATION

The true measure of a man's worth is not always the number of his friends, but sometimes the number of his foes. Every man who lives in advance of his age is sure to be misunderstood and opposed and often persecuted and sacrificed. The Lord himself has said: "Woe unto you, when all men shall speak well of you." "Marvel not, my brethren, if the world hate you." "If ye were of the world, the world would love his own."

Like Jesus, therefore, we must expect often to be unpopular, often to stand alone, even to be maligned; perhaps to be bitterly and falsely assailed and driven "without the camp" even of the religious world. Let us not be afraid to be unpopular, and let us never be soured or embittered by it. Let us stand sweetly and triumphantly in the confidence of right and of our Master's approval.

THE SUFFERING LIFE

No character is mature, no life has reached its coronation, until it has passed through fire. And so the supreme test of Christ's example was suffering, and in all His sufferings He has, as the apostle Peter expressed it, "left us an example that we should follow His steps" (1 Peter 2:21).

He suffered from the temptations of Satan for He "was in all points tempted like as we are, yet without sin." In this He has called us to follow Him in suffering and victory: "for in that he himself hath suffered being tempted, he is able to succour them that are tempted" (Hebrews 2:18). He suffered from the wrongs of men, and in this He has left us an example of patience, gentleness and forgiveness. "When he was reviled, reviled not again; when he suffered, he threatened not; but committed himself to him that judgeth righteously" (1 Peter 2:23).

Never was Jesus more glorious than in the hour of shame. Never was He more unselfish than in the moment when His own sorrows were crushing His heart. Never was He more victorious than when He bowed His head on the bitter cross and died for sinful men. He is the crowned Sufferer of humanity, and He calls us to suffer with Him in sweetness, submission and triumphant faith and love.

THE FINER TOUCHES OF HOLY CHARACTER

The perfection of character is to be found in the finer touches of temper and quality which easily escape the careless observer. It is in these that the character of Christ stands inimitably supreme.

One of the finest portraits of His spirit is given by Paul in the second chapter of Philippians as he tells us of His humility which might have grasped at His divine rights, but voluntarily surrendered them, emptied Himself and gladly stooped to the lowest place (Philippians 2:5-8). His unselfishness in dealing with the weak and the arrogant is finely expressed in "For even Christ pleased not himself; but, as it is written, The reproaches of them that reproached thee fell on me" (Romans 15:1, 3, 7). His gentleness and lowliness is finely expressed in His own words, "Learn of me; for I am meek and lowly in heart" (Matthew 11:29).

The highest element of character is self-sacrifice, and here the Master stands forever in the front of all sacrifice and heroism. "If any man will come after me, let him deny himself, and take up his cross, and follow me" (Matthew 16:24). "Whosoever will be chief among you, let him be your servant: Even as the Son of Man came not to be ministered unto, but to minister, and to give his life a ransom for many" (Matthew 20:27-28). Here we are taught what it means to walk even as He walked. It is the surrendered life. It is the life of self-sacrifice. So the apostle Paul has finely expressed it: "Walk in love, as Christ also hath loved us, and hath given himself for us an offering and a sacrifice to God for a sweet-smelling savour" (Ephesians 5:2). This is love, self-sacrifice, and this is to God as sweet as the fragrance of the gardens of Paradise.

There was something in the spirit of Jesus, and there ought to be something in every consecrated life, which can only be expressed by the word sweetness. It is with reference to this that the apostle says in 2 Corinthians 2:15: "We are unto God a sweet savour of Christ, in them that are saved, and in them that perish." May God give to us this heavenly sweetness that breathes from the heart of our indwelling Savior.

The refinement of Jesus Christ is one of the most striking traits of His lovely character. Untrained in the schools of human culture, He was notwithstanding as every Christian ought to be, a perfect gentleman. His thoughtful consideration of others is often manifest in the incidental circumstances of His life. For example, when Simon Peter was distressed about the tribute money at Capernaum, and was hesitating to speak to the Master about it, the Lord anticipated his very thought, and sent him down to the lake to catch the fish with the coin in its mouth. Then He added with fine tact, "That take, and give unto them for me and thee." He assumed the responsibility of the debt first for Himself to save Peter's sensitiveness.

Still finer was His high courtesy toward the poor sinning woman whom the Pharisees had dragged before Him. Stooping down, He evaded her glance lest she should be humiliated before them, and as though He did not hear them, He finally thrust a dart of holy sarcasm into their consciences which scattered them like hounds from His presence. Only when they were gone did He look up into that trembling woman's face and gently say, "Neither do I condemn thee: go, and sin no more" (John 8:11). So let us reflect the gentleness and courtesy of Christ, and not only by our lives but by our "manner of love" commend our Christianity and adorn the doctrine of God our Savior in all things.

There is one thing more in the spirit of the Master which He would have us copy, and that is the spirit of gladness. While the Lord Jesus was never hilarious or unrestrained in the expression of His joy, He was cheerful, bright and glad, and the heart in which He dwells should likewise be expressed in the shining face, the springing step, and the life of overflowing gladness.

There is nothing more needed in a sad and sinful world than joyous Christians. There was nothing more touching in the Master's life than when His own heart was ready to break with the anticipation of the garden and the cross, He was saying to them "Let not your heart be troubled" (John 14:27). "That my joy might remain in you, and that your joy might be full" (John 15:11). May God help us to copy the gladness of Jesus, never to droop our colors in the dust, never to hang our harps upon the willows, never to lose our heavenly blessing or fail to "rejoice evermore."

ELEMENTS OF POWER IN THE LIFE OF JESUS

It is possible to be sweet and good and yet to be weak and unwise. This was not the character of Jesus. Never was gentleness more childlike, never was manhood more mighty and majestic. In every element of His character, in every action of His life we see the strongest virility and we recognize continually that the Son of man was indeed a man in every sense of the word.

Intellectually His mind was clear and masterful. There is nothing finer in the story of His life than the calm, victorious way in which He answered the keen-witted lawyers and scribes who hounded Him with their questions. They were successively humiliated and silenced before the jeering crowd until they were glad to escape from His presence and after that ask Him no more questions.

So majestic and impressive was Jesus' eloquence that the officers who were sent to arrest Him forgot all about their commission as they stood listening to His wonderful words. They went back to their angry masters to exclaim "Never man spake like this Man."

There was a dignity about Him which sometimes rose to such a height that we read on one occasion as He set His face steadfastly to go to Jerusalem, "Jesus went before them: and they were amazed; and as they followed, they were afraid" (Mark 10:32). In the darkest hour of His agony He reached such a height of holy dignity that even Pilate gazed with admiration and pointing to Him amid all the symbols of shame and suffering cried, "Behold the Man." Even in His death He was a Conqueror, and in His resurrection and ascension He arose sublime above all the powers of death and hell.

How then shall we walk like Him?

1. We must receive Him to walk in us for He has said, "I will dwell in them and walk in them."

2. We must study His life until the story is burned into our consciousnesses and impressed upon our hearts.

3. We must constantly look upon the picture and apply it to every detail of our own conduct and so "beholding as in a glass the glory of the Lord, are changed into the same image from glory to glory, even as by the Spirit of the Lord" (2 Corinthians 3: 18).

4. We must not be discouraged when we meet with failure in ourselves. We must not be afraid to look in the glass and see our own defects in contrast with His blameless life. It will incite us to higher things. Self-judgment is the very secret of progress and higher attainment.

5. Finally, let us ask the Holy Spirit whose work it is to make Jesus real to us to unveil the vision and imprint the copy upon our hearts and lives. So shall we be "changed into the same image from glory to glory, even as by the Spirit of the Lord."

6

Kept

For I know whom I have believed, and am persuaded that he is able to keep that which I have committed unto him against that day (2 Timothy 1:12).
Kept by the power of God through faith unto salvation (1 Peter 1:5).

The more precious any treasure is, the more important is it that it be guarded and kept. The figure of our first text is that of a bank deposit and literally reads, "He is able to keep my deposits against that day." When great sums of gold are being conveyed to the vaults of some wealthy bank, squadrons of police may be on hand, and the most impregnable locks, bolts, bars and walls guard the treasure.

Sometimes the figure is used in a military sense. The second text is of this kind and literally should be translated, "Who are garrisoned by the power of God through faith unto salvation." What expenditures and armaments are employed to garrison the great strategic points that guard the gates of nations!

Sometimes the figure is used of the shepherd and his flock, "He that scattereth Israel will gather him, and keep him, as a shepherd doth his flock" (Jeremiah 31:10).

But whatever figure or phrase may be employed, the one great thought that God would convey to the hearts of His tried and suffering people is that they are safe in His keeping. He is able to guard that which we have committed unto Him against that day. Let us look at some of His gracious promises to keep His people.

1. *He will keep us wherever we may go or be.* Listen to the first promise of our Divine Keeper as it was addressed to Jacob in the hour of his loneliness and fear, "Behold, I am with thee, and will keep thee in all places whither thou goest . . . for I will not leave thee, until I have done that which I have spoken to thee of" (Genesis 28:15). How He kept that word to Jacob! In many places, providence cast his lot. The land of Laban, the cities of the Shechemites, the land of Goshen—everywhere his covenant-God guarded and kept him.

Jacob was not an attractive figure, he was not deserving of any special consideration. He was the "worm Jacob," but God loved him in His infinite grace and kept him, disciplined him, taught him and prepared him to be the head of Israel's tribes. The day came when Jacob could say, "The God which fed me all my life long unto this day, the angel which redeemed me from all evil" (Genesis 48:15-16).

Sometimes we may be in strange places, lonely places, hard places, dangerous places; but if we have taken Jacob's God as our covenant-God, we can rest without a fear in that ancient word, "Behold, I am with thee, and will keep thee in all places whither thou goest . . . for I will not leave thee, until I have done that which I have spoken to thee of" (Genesis 28:15).

> *To me remains nor place nor time,*
> *My country is in every clime,*
> *I can be calm and free from care*
> *On any shore, since God is there.*
>
> *Could I be cast where Thou art not,*
> *That were, indeed, a dreadful lot,*
> *But regions none remote I call,*
> *Secure of finding God in all.*

2. *He will keep us as the apple of His eye.* "Keep me as the apple of the eye" (Psalms 17:8). This is a beautiful figure illustrating the sensitiveness of the eye to the approach of any intruding particle. Instinctively the eyelid closes before the object can enter. There is no time to think, for the action is intuitive and involuntary.

The psalmist writes that we are as near to God as our eye is to us, and as much a part of the body of Christ as if it were really the crystalline lens of His very eyes. He is as sensitive to the approach of anything that could harm us as we would be to the intrusion of a grain of dust to our sensitive eye.

> *God is the refuge of His saints,*
> > *When storms of sharp distress invade;*
> *Ere we can offer our complaint,*
> > *Behold Him present with His aid.*

3. *He will keep us in His pavilion.* "Thou shalt hide them in the secret of thy presence from the pride of

man: thou shalt keep them secretly in a pavilion
from the strife of tongues" (Psalms 31:20). It does not
take God long to erect that pavilion in the most soli-
tary place and hide His children safely within its cur-
tains.

The story is told of a Scottish assembly of faithful
worshipers in one of the glens when the cruel
Claverhouse was hunting for the blood of the saints.
Suddenly the cry was made from the sentinel watch-
ing on a neighboring cliff that soldiers were coming.
The little company had been discovered.

Escape was impossible. The Christians just knelt
down and prayed, claiming this precious psalm,
"Thou shalt hide them in Thy pavilion." Immediately there began to gather among the hills a thick
Scotch mist, and everything was enveloped as in a
curtain. Their enemies were baffled, and the believers quietly escaped through the familiar path-
ways of the mountains. God had hidden them securely in His pavilion.

We may not have the same bloody foe as the Scottish Covenanters, but a wicked tongue sustains a
sharper sword and crueler hate. How often we find
the psalmist calling out against the envenomed words
of men: "What shall be given unto thee? or what shall
be done unto thee, thou false tongue? Sharp arrows
of the mighty, with coals of juniper" (Psalms 120:3-
4). But He can shield us even from these and give us a
blessing for every bitter blast from human slander.

"Let him curse," said David when they tried to
quiet old Shimei who was abusing the king in the
hour of his sorrow; "it may be . . . that the Lord will
requite me good for his cursing this day" (2 Samuel

16:11-12). "Wherefore let them that suffer according to the will of God commit the keeping of their souls to him in well doing, as unto a faithful creator" (1 Peter 4:19).

4. *He will keep us in perfect peace.* "Thou wilt keep him in perfect peace, whose mind is stayed on thee: because he trusteth in thee" (Isaiah 26:3). Literally this reads, "Peace, peace." It is the double peace *with* God and *of* God. It is the Old Testament original of the apostle's still more beautiful promise, "Be careful for nothing; but in every thing by prayer and supplication with thanksgiving let your requests be made known unto God. And the peace of God, which passeth all understanding, shall keep your hearts and minds through Christ Jesus" (Philippians 4:6-7).

In both verses it is the same peace which is referred to, that deep, divine rest which Christ puts into the heart where He comes to dwell. It is the peace of God, and it passes all understanding. It is not the result of reasoning or sight. It is not because things have changed and we can see the deliverance coming. It comes when all is dark and strange and we have nothing but His bare word.

Sennacherib, the king of Assyria, was at the gates of Jerusalem, and there seemed no possible escape when the voice of the prophet said, "Be strong and courageous, be not afraid nor dismayed for the king of Assyria, nor for all the multitude that is with him: for there be more with us than with him: With him is an arm of flesh; but with us is the Lord our God to help us, and to fight our battles" (2 Chronicles 32: 7-8). And then it is added, "The people rested themselves." The Assyrian was still there and the danger was just as imminent, but there came upon them an unreasoning and supernatural confidence, for God had undertaken their defense.

We know the sequel. How easy it was for Jehovah by the touch of a single angel's hand to lay those mighty hosts silent in the dust! So God's peace comes not by sight, but by faith. Its conditions are, "Thou wilt keep him in perfect peace, whose mind is stayed on thee, because he trusteth in thee."

Someone tells of two competing paintings of peace for which a great prize was offered. One was of a beautiful and tranquil scene, a woodland valley with a gentle stream softly winding through grassy banks. There were warbling birds and happy, playing children with the flocks lying down in green pastures. Earth and heaven were at rest. The other—the picture that won the prize—was of a raging sea flinging high its billows and its foam around a naked rock. A ship in the distance was driving before the hurricane with every sail furled, and seabirds whirled through the leaden clouds in wild confusion. It seemed to be anything but peace. But far up in a cleft of that naked rock, above the surf and sheltered from the storm, there was a dove's nest with the mother quietly spreading her soft wings above her young in perfect peace.

When is the time to trust?
   Is it when all is calm?
When waves the victor's palm
And life is one great psalm
   Of peace and rest?
No! But the time to trust
   Is when the waves beat high,

> *And storm clouds sweep the sky,*
> *And faith can only cry,*
>   *Lord help and save.*

The beautiful figure of the text in Philippians is that of a garrison, the peace of God which garrisons the heart and mind. The need of the garrison here is not because of outside but inside foes. Nothing can harm us from the outside if we are kept in God's perfect peace.

Notice also that there are two sections of this citadel that have to be garrisoned and guarded. One is the heart, the seat of doubts and fears and cares. The other is the mind where our thoughts become the sources of unrest, and we wonder and worry and look forward and back and everywhere but to God. The peace of God can quiet all our thinking and hold us in stillness and sweetly say to us,

> *Cease your thinking, troubled Christian,*
>   *What avail your anxious cares?*
> *God is ever thinking for you;*
>   *Jesus ev'ry burden bears.*
> *Casting all your care upon Him,*
>   *Sink into His blessed will*
> *While He folds you to His bosom,*
>   *Sweetly whisp'ring, "Peace, be still."*

5. *He will keep us by His power.* This is the meaning of our second text—"Garrisoned by the power of God through faith unto salvation." The apostle has just told us that the inheritance is kept for us in heaven. Now he tells us we are kept for the inheritance. The inheritance is reserved for us, and we are preserved

for the inheritance.

But while the figure of the garrison is the same as in Philippians, yet it is a different garrison. There it was peace, now it is power. The garrison of peace is to preserve the city from internal foes; the garrison of power is to protect it from its outward enemies. The one garrison polices the streets; the other mans the walls. And it adds to the force of the figure to note that the word *power* here in the Greek is *dynamite.* The garrison is armed with heavenly artillery.

When first the English troops under Lord Kitchener met the vast armies of the Mahdi, the conquering leader of the fanatical hordes of the Sudan who outnumbered them ten to one, they protected their camp by modern artillery while the Africans came against them with old-fashioned muskets and rifles. A hundred thousand strong, that vast array hurled itself upon the little company of English soldiers and marched to the assault with flying banners, galloping horses, and splendid enthusiasm.

The historian graphically tells how quietly and confidently the English waited the onset, for they knew that they had power in their midst before which those legions could not for a moment stand. Suddenly the Maxim guns began their terrific rattle, and like a hailstorm from the heavens a rain of bullets and shells was poured upon the black host, who melted like snow before a summer sun. It was dynamite against mere human courage.

God has garrisoned us with heavenly dynamite, the power of the Holy Spirit, and, like the English soldiers, we must have confidence in it, for we are kept by the dynamite of God through faith. We must count upon His mighty strength and always go forth with the battle cry, "Thanks be unto God, which always causeth us to triumph" (2 Corinthians 2:14).

6. *He is able to keep us in the world and from the evil.* This was the Master's prayer for His disciples. In John 17:15 we read, "I pray not that thou shouldest take them out of the world, but that thou shouldest keep them from the evil." Here is a double keeping. Kept from death and sickness and anything that could take us out of the world, and yet kept from the evil of the world and especially the evil one. In the original language it is the Evil One.

This is no abstract evil, but a great personal devil—the adversary who "as a roaring lion, walketh about, seeking whom he may devour" (1 Peter 5:8). But the Lord's power and the Lord's keeping stand between us and his devouring jaws. He is a conquered foe, and we are to treat him as such and to go forth against him with the prestige of a victor in the name of his Conqueror, the Lord Jesus Christ.

Sometimes the devil assails us by his wiles and sometimes by his fiery darts, but with the shield of faith we shall be able to stand against them both. We must not be too afraid of the devil. Some people get so afraid of him that they almost fear to let the Lord have right of way in His own meetings. The dread of fanaticism has kept a good many well-meaning people from the baptism of the Holy Spirit. Let us boldly come and take all God has for us and trust Him to keep the counterfeit away.

If we ask bread, God is not going to give us a stone, and if we ask fish and really want what He wants, He will not let us have a serpent. In the name of Jesus and through His precious blood, we shall be safe and kept from the evil one.

7. *He is able to keep us from stumbling.* Jude says, "Now unto him that is able to keep you from falling, and to present you faultless before the presence of his glory with exceeding joy" (Jude 1:24). The English translation is inadequate. The word *falling* means *stumbling.* Of course He is able to keep us from being lost. Too many Christians are content to just get through, if it be by the skin of their teeth. That is a poor, ignoble ambition. He is able to keep us even from stumbling and to present us faultless before the presence of His glory with exceeding joy.

If God is able to keep us for one second, He can keep us for 33 million seconds—one whole year—and as much longer as we keep trusting Him moment by moment. Let us rise to a higher ambition and allow Him to keep us even from slipping, tripping and stumbling.

8. *He is able to keep us from the touch of the adversary.* There is a fine promise in the last chapter of First John. "He that is begotten of God keepeth himself, and that wicked one toucheth him not" (1 John 5:18). The only begotten Son keeps the saint who trusts Him and so keeps him that the wicked one cannot touch him.

It is the old familiar picture of the fly on one side of the window and the bird on the other. The bird dashes for its prey and thinks it has it. The fly shudders and thinks so too, but there is a thud and some flustered feathers and a badly frightened bird, but the fly is still there, wondering how he escaped being swallowed up. But to us the secret is all plain: there was something between the bird and fly that the bird did not see and the fly had forgotten.

Thank God, when the devil makes his fiercest dives, there is Someone between him and us. He has to get through Jesus Christ to get us. If we only abide in simple confidence, the devil will get a good deal more hurt than we.

9. *He is able to keep His servants and ministers.* Listen! "I the Lord have called thee in righteousness, and will hold thine hand, and will keep thee, and give thee for a covenant of the people, for a light of the Gentiles" (Isaiah 42:6). This blessed promise belongs primarily to the Lord Jesus, but secondarily to every other true servant of Jehovah who is abiding in Him and working for Him.

God holds His ministers in His right hand and says, "Touch not mine anointed, and do my prophets no harm" (1 Chronicles 16:22). He is a very reckless man who speaks lightly or acts against any true servant of the Lord. We must be careful how we criticize the Master's servants. "Who art thou that judgest another man's servant? to his own master he standeth or falleth . . . for God is able to make him stand" (Romans 14:4).

"Who art thou that judgest another?" If we are serving Christ with a true heart, we need not be afraid. He whom the Father beholds will hold our right hands and keep us and say to us, "I have loved thee: therefore will I give men for thee, and people for thy life" (Isaiah 43:4). "I will work and who shall let it?" (Isaiah 43:13). God will say to us, "I have covered thee in the shadow of mine hand, that I may plant the heavens, and lay the foundations of the earth, and say to Zion, Thou art my people" (Isaiah 51:16).

A single soldier of the cross standing for Jesus and trusting in Him is mightier than legions of powerful foes. Let us trust Him though dangers and foes surround us and friends may often be few. The heavens will fall and earth be dissolved before He can fail one of His trusting servants.

10. *He will keep His cause, His Church, His vineyard.* "Sing ye unto her, A vineyard of red wine. I the Lord do keep it; I will water it every moment: lest any hurt it, I will keep it night and day" (Isaiah 27:2-3). We sometimes believe that we are the keepers of God's cause and that He has forgotten all about it. We feel we have to shout and cry to get Him to help us look after His own property. Why, the Lord is looking after us and the cause too. "I, the Lord, do keep it . . . lest any hurt it, I will keep it night and day."

No doubt there are dangers, trials, adversaries, but there is one thing more: the Lord. And two little words are stronger than all the *Ds* in the dictionary, whether they be difficulty, discouragement, division, declension, the devil. Those two words are *but God.*

There is a fine prophetic picture in the opening verses of Zechariah that was written to comfort people in troubled times. First the prophet saw four horns coming from all directions—sharp, cruel, powerful horns. They were pushing and piercing everything before them. If he looked north, there was a horn there, and south, there was another there. They were soon to meet, and he would find himself between the two. If he looked east, there was a horn there, and west, there was another there, and they were meeting in his unprotected breast.

Then the scene changed, and he looked and saw four carpenters coming in the same directions. Each of them had tools—a stout ax, a sharp saw and no doubt a heavy maul. Soon he heard the blows of axes and the buzzing of saws, and the horns had lost their points and were pounded to a jelly and were soft cushions that could not hurt anything.

God has a carpenter for every horn and if the work we are doing is His work, the gates of hell cannot prevail against it.

God is able to keep everything that we commit to Him. "I know whom I have believed. and am persuaded that he is able to keep that which I have committed unto him against that day" (2 Timothy 1:12). The great question is this: How much have we really committed?